It's Happening with Youth

It's Happening with Youth

Janice M. Corbett & Curtis E. Johnson

1817

HARPER & ROW, PUBLISHERS

New York · Evanston · San Francisco · London

Framingham State College
Framingham, Massachusetts

IT'S HAPPENING WITH YOUTH. Copyright © 1972 by Janice M. Corbett and Curtis E. Johnson. All rights reserved. Printed in the United States of America. No part of this book may be used or reproduced in any manner whatsoever without written permission except in the case of brief quotations embodied in critical articles and reviews. For information address Harper & Row, Publishers, Inc., 49 East 33rd Street, New York, N.Y. 10016. Published simultaneously in Canada by Fitzhenry & Whiteside Limited, Toronto.

FIRST EDITION

LIBRARY OF CONGRESS CATALOG CARD NUMBER: 79-183632

Contents

PREFACE   viii

MEANINGS AND METHODS

Chapter 1   The Crisis in Youth Ministry   2
Chapter 2   The Response to the Crisis   12
Chapter 3   The Youth Ministry Process   22

THE MINISTRIES

Chapter 4   Camden Youth Ministry, Camden, New
            Jersey   38
Chapter 5   Telegraph Avenue Ministry, Berkeley,
            California   45
Chapter 6   The Community, Oberlin, Ohio   59
Chapter 7   The Catacombs, Ventura, California   68
Chapter 8   Operation Bridge, Omaha, Nebraska   77
Chapter 9   Provadenic, Cleveland, Ohio   85
Chapter 10 The Way, Quincy, Massachusetts   96
Chapter 11 Black Culture Center, Indianapolis, In-
            diana   104

Chapter 12	Beechview Community Youth Program, Pittsburgh, Pennsylvania	111
Chapter 13	Two Rural Ministries: Timber Lake, South Dakota, and North Livermore, Maine	119
Chapter 14	Summer Lawn-In, Melrose, Massachusetts	129
Chapter 15	The Peace Pipers, Ravenna, Ohio	136
Chapter 16	Kamp Kachess, Easton, Washington	142
Chapter 17	"Somebody Cares" Hotline, Silver Spring, Maryland	148

THE FUTURE

Chapter 18	Conflict with the Institutional Church	156
Appendix A	Human Relations Training Organizations	166
Appendix B	Action Training Organizations	170
Appendix C	Sources of Information on Foundation Grants	174

Preface

Preface

This book began as a personal search for a relevant youth ministry.

We had worked with youth during the turbulent sixties and had become frustrated with a traditional ministry that seemed unrelated to the crises faced by youth in their changing world.

When we moved to a denominational youth ministry staff, we had a chance to see some more relevant models of ministry at first hand. And as we traveled to various parts of the country, we discovered the methods and structures we had been searching for earlier.

It soon became obvious that many persons were as unaware of these models as we had been, for several reasons. Some ministries had moved outside the institutional church and information about them was not available through normal church communication channels. Others developed as ecumenical ministries and ecumenical communication channels are limited. All of the ministries were quite new and, in many cases, people had not yet discovered that they existed.

The book attempts to describe some of these new youth ministries for others who face the frustration we faced. It also tries to assist those who want to create new youth ministries in their own churches.

It is not our intent to "put down" traditional youth ministries. In many places they are still serving a valid purpose. Instead, we have tried to offer alternatives to those who want to go beyond the ministry in which they are presently involved to create new forms for a new generation.

The case studies that make up the main portion of the book are based on personal interviews and visits. (Only two ministries were not visited personally: Beechview Community Youth Program and Kamp Kachess. However, personal interviews were conducted with people involved in these two programs.)

We are convinced that personal contact is the best means of learning about the process of creating new forms of youth ministry. So we would urge you to seek out new youth ministries in your own area, to talk with persons involved in them, work with them, and learn from them.

In this fast-changing world, many of the forms of youth ministry described in this book may be radically changed or even disappear by the time these words come into print. But the process that persons used to develop these ministries and the insights they had will, we believe, be relevant for a long time.

Finally, we would like to stress that all opinions in this book are our own. In no case do they represent policies of agencies by which we are or have been employed.

Meanings and Methods

CHAPTER 1

The Crisis in Youth Ministry

Meher Baba is here, now, to unite us all in love. baba is the avatar, god-man, he was christ, budda, mohammed; he is all, he asks for nothing but your love and to love baba is to love everything. all paths lead to god and baba is here to help us. to find god, you must look in your heart and seek your true self the inner self that is one with god . . . i am only trying to say that all truth lies with yourself.
—William Ward
From *Helix*, an underground newspaper published in Seattle, Washington.

Declarations like the above, found in underground newspapers, on subway walls, and in paperback best sellers, are challenging the Christian church to take a new look at its ministry with youth.

A generation has emerged among us that is seeking spiritual renewal, but it is conducting its search almost entirely outside the institutional church's walls. Zen Buddhist cults, astrology devotees, "Jesus Freaks," drug cults—all seek means of saving themselves and their world, with little reference to the traditional religious structures that have for so long been considered repositories of our culture's spiritual values.

How did this phenomenon come about? How did the church lose touch with this generation? Does the church have anything to say that is relevant to youth in today's world? Do youth have anything to say to the church? If so, how can communication be reestablished?

A Youth Ministry Crisis

The alienation of youth from the church did not happen overnight. But it has only reached crisis proportions in the last decade. To understand why, it is necessary to review the development of the church's ministry with youth.

Youth ministry, as a specialized function of the church, had its beginnings in the Industrial Revolution. Before that time, the church was a family organization with few activities designed for exclusive age groupings.

Industrialization, immigration, and urbanization spawned what Margaret Mead describes as a "cofigurative culture."[1] This is a culture in which children model their behavior on that of their peers rather than on that of their parents and grandparents. It is a culture in which adolescents are expected to learn from each other and to develop their own culture.

As this peer culture assumed increasing importance, the church began to focus attention upon it. The church's concern was twofold. On the one hand, it was concerned that youth adopt its values and find the "abundant life" it had to offer. On the other hand, it viewed youth as an investment it had to nurture in order to insure its institutional survival.

Large youth organizations emerged as the predominant form of this early youth ministry. Originating in small, diverse, local organizations (Sunday school classes, the "young people's society," missionary groups), these large organizations encompassed all of the youth activities of the church and developed

---

1. Margaret Mead, *Culture and Commitment, a Study of the Generation Gap* (Garden City, N. Y.: Natural History Press/Doubleday & Co. 1970), p. 52.

into highly structured national bodies. In many ways, they became a youth church, reaching their zenith in the 1940s and early 1950s.

The national youth organizations reflected the church's concern, in that period, with its institutional life. Youth members developed a loyalty to the institutional church that had seldom before been witnessed. They wore the church's symbols, chanted its pledges, and worked hard to bring more members into its fold. In the process, many found meaning for their lives and shared it with others.

The turbulent sixties called these massive youth organizations into question. Confrontation with racism, war, poverty, the mass media revolution, the sexual revolution, drugs, the technological revolution, and all of the social ills exposed during those traumatic years brought youth organizations, along with the whole institutional church, into judgment. And the youth organizations were forced to admit that they had become self-serving. They saw their mission and recognized that they had failed to fulfill it. And they questioned whether their organizations could ever fulfill it, as they were then structured.

At the same time, youth culture was developing into a recognizable subculture, with its own language, symbols, dress, and values. We were into what Margaret Mead describes as the "prefigurative age," when adults actually learn from their children.[2] Youth were finding some ways of living in today's world that adults had not yet discovered. They had recaptured some of the values adults had lost. And they challenged the church to let them shape their own ministry.

But while youth were creating a culture for a new age, adults were retreating into whatever security they could find in their trauma-filled world. This security was most often found in their institutions, including the church. Many already had an intense institutional loyalty because they had grown up in the youth organizations of the forties that fostered such loyalty. So the

---

2. *Ibid.*, p. 1.

search for security, coupled with a profound institutional loyalty, forced adults into rigid positions within the church. Doctrine became sacred. Buildings took on added importance. And adults came into open conflict with youth, who challenged their institutions and values.

This conflict is at the heart of the youth ministry crisis today. Adults are not willing to admit that youth have needs they might not have had—and answers they have not yet found. Youth are not willing to admit that adults have some of the very values they are seeking.

So churches continue to sponsor adult-dominated youth organizations, or to force unquestioned doctrine on apathetic youth, or to abdicate to entertainment and recreation programs that will "keep youth in the church."

And so youth are seeking their spiritual answers outside the institution.

A Relevant Youth Ministry

Assuming that spiritual meaning relevant to today's world can be found within the Christian religion—and we make this assumption after much soul-searching—what can churches do to share in the search for faith with youth?

Several things have been suggested by observers of the youth ministry scene. We will review these suggestions as a means of describing the basic principles underlying the youth ministries described later in this book.

Essentially, the church that wants to communicate with youth must do three things. It must communicate with, not to youth. It must redefine its message in terms of today's realities. And it must know, understand, and love the youth with whom it is communicating.

In addition, the church must make some radical structural changes if it is to share its ministry with youth. These changes are described in detail in the final chapter.

WITH, NOT TO YOUTH

To understand the importance of communicating with youth —that is, to carry on a two-way communication in which adults and youth both learn from and teach each other—we must recognize that a generation gap does in fact exist.

Margaret Mead says: "True communication becomes possible only when both realize that they speak not one, but two languages in which the 'same' words have divergent, sometimes radically different meanings. . . . Once the fact of a deep, new unprecedented world-wide generation gap is firmly established, in the minds of both the young and the old, communication can be established again."[3]

Once the gap is recognized, we must seek ways to bridge it. We must establish environments in which both generations can feel comfortable. We must establish climates of respect between the generations. And, above all, we must learn to listen.

It is probably harder for adults to make these adjustments than for youth. We lived through an adolescence in which our opinions were not sought and our ideas were not heard. It is natural for us to want to put youth through the same experience. And many of us really do not respect the ideas of youth. We question how they could possibly know as much or more than we do. After all, they have only lived half as long.

We fail to see that youth have experienced a world we never knew. They have learned modern math and space science. They have used computers and videotape. They have seen war on television and racial violence in their schools. They have reaped the rewards of materialism and experienced our nation's spiritual decay. In many ways, they have lived in the world of the present much more than we. They can help us put our world together—and apply our faith to it—through their perspective on the "now."

3. *Ibid.*, p. 80.

Youth, on the other hand, need to learn to appreciate the world we have experienced. They need to know that materialism did not grow in a vacuum; it was nurtured by economic deprivation. They need to appreciate the meaning of technological advances for persons who worked on mass-production lines at demeaning tasks twelve hours a day.

Youth need to appreciate the vision our prophets of the past have had, even as they challenge our generation to live up to the values it preaches. We can learn from each other, and we need to establish climates where this is possible.

REDEFINING OUR MESSAGE

One of the hardest tasks facing the church that wants to establish a relevant ministry with youth is the task of restating its theology in terms that are appropriate to this generation's understanding of its world.

This need became clear to us as we talked with a group of youth in a moderate-sized East Coast city a year ago. We were taping an interview with youth who were "alienated" from the church. We expected them to say that the church's hymns were slow and its sermons dull. Instead, they talked about the church's theology. Over and over they expressed a desire for the church to say something meaningful. They didn't buy the grandfatherly God of their childhood Sunday school classes. They didn't buy the Puritan sex ethic. They didn't buy a heaven for good people and a hell for bad. They wanted the church to answer the hard questions they were posing about meaning in their world today.

It is hard for the church to admit that its doctrines may not be relevant. But if it is to communicate with youth, the church must confront its doctrines honestly in the harsh light of human experience in a technological age.

This is not the first time that the church's theology has been questioned. The Reformation was a major theological revolution growing out of an era of massive social change. Many have called the present "renewal" of the church a New Reformation. But in many churches, this renewal has been an action-oriented movement, with an underdeveloped and poorly articulated theological base. Youth are calling the church to honestly examine its doctrines and to create a new theology that is appropriate for a new age.

KNOWING YOUTH

And the church must know, understand, and love the youth with whom it is attempting to communicate.

To know and love youth is to discover them as individuals. Youth at an intergenerational conference we attended pleaded with the leaders to be called by their names, not constantly referred to as "the youth."

At the same time, however, it is important to understand youth in the context of their culture. We have referred earlier to this culture as a subculture. It exists within our common culture but has characteristics that set it apart.

Some of these characteristics are easily observed: long hair, rock music, jeans, the use of drugs. Other characteristics are not so easily observed. These are the values and perspectives youth use to guide their actions in the world.

Some of these values and perspectives are, according to Reich: a sense of personal worth and personal responsibility, a sense of living in the "now" rather than the past or future, a sense of openness to all experience, and a rejection of any imposed system of belief.[4]

These values and perspectives are, we believe, common to most youth in America today. We often fail to recognize this, particularly if we are working with youth in the 12-to18-year-old age bracket (as do most people who work with youth in the church).

---

4. Charles A. Reich, *The Greening of America* (New York: Random House, 1970).

The Crisis in Youth Ministry

Persons in this age group are usually not full members of the subculture that has been labeled "youth culture." To be full members, they must have a degree of independence from their parents, and most junior high and high school youth have not yet reached this stage. They may imitate the dress and hair styles of the youth culture, listen to its music, experiment with its drugs, and even live with its members on weekends. But it will not become their life-style until they are free from dependency needs enough to adopt a life-style of their own.

But even though they are not full members of the youth culture, these youth in their teens are on their way to achieving full membership. They are learning much more and accepting much more from the youth culture than they are from the culture of their parents. They may already be viewing their world from the perspectives described by Reich, and the church that is operating from a different perspective—such as the church that emphasizes a good life in the hereafter rather than now—makes little sense to them.

An important part of understanding this subculture is recognizing that the term "youth culture" is often applied to groupings of young people that are quite different. While most youth share the values and perspectives described above, and even some of the outward manifestations of the youth culture, they work out their life-styles in several different kinds of groupings. There are a number of these groupings, and they are constantly changing. But some that we feel have achieved a degree of permanence in the last five years, and for which the church has had to find different forms of ministry, are street youth, ethnic cults, Establishment youth, the "Silent Majority," and counter-culture youth.

Street youth may either be runaways or youth who have left home with their parents' permission and are simply bumming around. They live on the streets, often near university communities. They are often on drugs and are dependent on community resources for basic necessities, such as food and medical care. They are often alienated from traditional social structures.

Ethnic cults encompass youth who share the same ethnic background. Black youth were probable the first in our time to claim their heritage and attempt to preserve it in a cult. Since then, Hispanic youth cults have developed, along with Indian-American and others.

We use the term "Establishment youth" to describe those who hold onto such values as the good athlete–good student–good businessman syndrome, while at the same time adopting certain aspects of youth culture, particularly its music.

"Silent Majority" youth are traditionally found in the Midwest, although we have met them in eastern suburbs and West Coast cities. They have rejected the youth culture and tend to accept the values of the over-thirty generation. They wear their hair short, listen to country-and-western music, and join the Army when they are eighteen. In many cases, Silent Majority youth become the strongest converts to youth culture when they leave home. Often, they have not been free to experiment with their own life-styles before that time because of tightly controlled home environments.

Counter-culture youth are portrayed by the mass media as representing all youth today. They fit the stereotype called up by the term "youth culture." They are seriously engaged in what Roszak calls "the making of a counter culture."[5] Politically and socially aware, they may experiment with drugs and sex, sometimes live in communes, eat organic foods, and work at crafts rather than in industry. They are usually the trendsetters of youth culture today.

The church has spent most of its energies in developing a ministry for either the Establishment youth or the Silent Majority youth, and has had some degree of success in communicating with them. Other youth, however, have been alienated from the church, particularly those who are on the cutting edge of the counterculture. If the church is to be really relevant

---

5. Theodore Roszak, *The Making of a Counter Culture* (Garden City, N. Y.: Doubleday and Co., Inc., 1968).

to a changing world, it will have to develop communication with counterculture youth as well as with street youth, ethnic cults, and all other groupings that emerge.

Creating Relevant Ministries

There are some churches that have been able to understand today's youth, develop a relevant message, and communicate with them. This book describes a few such churches.

It also describes the process through which these churches have gone in creating a relevant ministry with a new generation. This process, we believe, can be applied in other churches. The next chapters describe how.

CHAPTER 2

The Response to the Crisis

The demise of most large youth organizations within the church in the sixties left a vacuum in youth ministry. While some churches have been able to continue strong programs along traditional youth organization lines, many have found these old patterns wanting and have floundered in a search for something new.

Here and there, churches have found the "something new" that works for them, and have created a new form of youth ministry. These new ministries are quite varied, ranging from communes to hot lines. But, for the purpose of our study, they might be divided into classes on the basis of their primary objective.

Types of New Youth Ministries

We have chosen to divide the new youth ministries into three classes: communities, youth services, and political action groups.

The objective of communities is to establish a closely knit group where persons can feel accepted and live out their Christian faith together.

Youth services provide youth with such things as medical aid, free food, housing, and counseling.

Political action groups attempt to change political structures so that they are more responsive to human needs.

COMMUNITIES

There are many kinds of communities. Kamp Kachess (chapter 16) is a residential home that helps alienated boys become full members of a Christian community. The commune in Camden (chapter 4) is also a residential center, but it is a place where people are trying to work out a new kind of social order.

Not all communities are residential. Some are simply drop-in centers, with very informal relationships. The Lawn-In (chapter 14) was probably the most informal drop-in community we visited.

Somewhere between residential centers and drop-in centers is The Way in Quincy, Massachusetts (chapter 10). This is a somewhat highly structured "home annex" that provides family security but does not remove youth from their home settings.

Some communities are still based on the youth organization model, as in Ravenna, Ohio (chapter 15). But there are important differences between the old organizations and the new. Youth play an important decision-making role in the new organizations; they are not adult-dominated. And the new organizations have a much more flexible structure. They may be organized around a coffee house one year and a service project the next. There is no set pattern of organization, as was true with the old officer-and-program-chairman model.

In many communities there is a definite progression from informal to more structured (yet still flexible) organization, so that the more mature communities seem to provide a balanced youth ministry that has developed through a natural maturing process.

This is illustrated by the Beechview Community Ministry (chapter 12), which began as a drop-in center, with informal recreation as the primary activity. Soon more structured recreation evolved in the form of dances and light shows. Then educational services emerged, with classes on police-youth relations and talks with mayoral candidates. Eventually the youth requested worship services, especially for special events like Moratorium Day.

The final stage of development in a community is when it reaches outside of itself to become involved in one of the other types of youth ministry, direct service or political action.

YOUTH SERVICES

Although mature youth communities may provide direct services, they are usually provided by adults. Generally, adults have more skill and time available for direct services than do youth. They can make the community contacts, organize volunteers, order supplies, and carry out the services, usually while youth are in school.

Another reason that adults usually provide direct services is that most of the services are provided for youth who are unable to help themselves or to become involved in helping others. And youth who are free of personal concerns enough to become involved in helping are not allowed to, because parents fear their association with the youth who are being serviced.

Some examples of youth ministries that provide direct services are the Telegraph Avenue Ministry in Berkeley (runaway center, food program, free clinic, housing, etc.; see chapter 5), Operation Bridge in Omaha (youth counseling; see chapter 8), Provadenic (medical services in Nicaragua; see chapter 9), and the Somebody Cares Hotline in Silver Spring, Maryland (chapter 17).

In many cases, the direct services develop into communities for the youth being serviced. Political action also develops as a side effect of some services, as they become involved with the symptoms of social injustice. But the primary objective of these groups remains to provide direct services to youth.

POLITICAL ACTION GROUPS

Youth political action groups are probably the newest form that youth ministry has taken in the last decade. They have developed in response to two factors: the church's rediscovery of its need to exert political pressure, and youth's own discovery of its ability to influence decisions affecting them.

Youth political action groups try to change political structures in their communities and in the country at large. The structure most often attacked is the school. However, groups have confronted church governing bodies, the federal government, draft boards, and other political structures.

One of the most effective youth political action groups we visited is Concerned Youth, an organization based in Rochester, New York. It developed out of a larger community ministry, RISK, and separated to form its own organization when its political activities became controversial and affected the financial stability of the larger organization.

Unfortunately, we were unable to describe Concerned Youth in this book because the group was in a transitional phase following the resignation of its first director, Mike Losinger. We discovered, however, that Mike and the Concerned Youth organization have had a tremendous influence on the development of other youth political action groups in churches. One of these, The Community in Oberlin, Ohio, is described in chapter 6.

Political action groups sometimes develop a strong sense of community (as evidenced by the name of the Oberlin group), but this is a side effect rather than a principal objective. As a matter of fact, there is something of a cliquishness about some political action groups. The youth have become "politically aware," and this sets them apart from other youth. They feel they are involved in the "revolution," and this sets them apart from many adults. Their conversation is full of terms that are unfamiliar to many youth and adults: "co-opting," and "politicizing," as well as some language that might be considered obscene. This also sets them apart.

Political action groups are seldom involved in direct services to youth. They consider direct service to be a Band-Aid approach that temporarily relieves symptoms but does not bring about the radical changes in structures they are fighting for.

Although political action groups are not organized to promote personal growth, this is also a side effect that sometimes emerges. Youth in political action groups develop a strong sense of their own power as well as a strong Christian commitment, and this enables them to grow into more effective individuals.

ACHIEVING A BALANCE

As indicated in these descriptions of new youth ministries, there is a great deal of overlapping of purposes. Communities become involved in direct service, youth services become involved in political action, and political action groups become communities.

Actually, all three are needed for a balanced youth ministry. All youth need opportunities for personal growth within accepting communities, opportunities for service, and opportunities for effecting change in society. Most groups will concentrate on one area at a time. But all three need to be available at some time in the church that is trying to provide a balanced youth ministry.

Characteristics of the New Ministries

Just as it is difficult to classify the new forms of ministry into distinct categories, it is difficult to pull out characteristics that describe them and set them apart from youth ministry of the past. But some generalizations can be made about the new ministries in terms of their perspectives, objectives, and operational procedures.

The Response to the Crisis

COMMUNITY-ORIENTED

Most new youth ministries involve both nonchurch and church youth, but the approach to nonchurch youth is different from what it has traditionally been.

In the past, the church sought out nonchurch youth in order to make them church youth. Today, churches are attempting to meet the needs of nonchurch youth without insisting that they first become church members. Youth and youth ministers are taking the church into the community rather than insisting that the community come into the church.

PERSON-ORIENTED

Many of the new youth ministries are person-oriented rather than institution-oriented. They are not concerned with perpetuating institutions, including the institutional church, unless these institutions are serving people.

A lack of emphasis on numbers is one result of this person-orientation. Many groups are purposely kept small so that personal needs can be met. The commune in Camden, for example, serves an average of seventeen permanent residents with a full-time director and a two-story building.

Even when large groups of persons are involved, as in the Lawn-in in Melrose, Massachusetts, or the Telegraph Avenue Ministry in Berkeley, an attempt is made to meet personal needs through a variety of activities and flexible programs.

A FULL-TIME DIRECTOR

Each ministry described here has a full-time director. This does not mean that all youth ministries must have a full-time director, but it is significant that many of the most relevant ones do. (Sometimes this director is a staff member of a church who has broader responsibilities, but who gives a major portion of his or her time to youth ministry.)

A full-time director is probably needed for two reasons: the nature of youth ministry and the scope of these projects.

Youth ministry has, for many years, been given marginal time in the church. Most of the energy of the professional staff has been spent in ministering with adults. Many people assumed that youth ministry was simply preparing youth to be future churchmen and hence the task could be assumed by volunteers who were themselves good churchmen.

Today, however, the concept of youth ministry has been enlarged. Youth are now (rightly) encouraged to minister in their present situation. The task of enabling them to understand their present situation and develop skills for ministering in it is much more complex.

In some cases it may be possible for part-time leaders to do this larger task. However, it is very rare for persons who are fully employed to have adequate time available.

Having a full-time director has many advantages. He is able to spend time with youth, to get to know their world. He can become their advocate with the rest of the church and community. He can be available whenever they need him for counseling. He can keep up to date with trends in youth culture and can become involved in continuing education experiences related to youth ministry.

In order to employ a full-time director, many churches have had to work ecumenically or work in cooperation with their communities. Or they have had to supplement their resources with government funds or privately solicited money.

ECUMENICAL

As stated above, many youth ministries have become ecumenical in order to finance the services of a full-time director. Others have become ecumenical as an outgrowth of the unifying spirit in the churches today.

Many churches feel it is essential to work ecumenically in

youth ministry to enable youth to develop a sense of unity with the whole church.

NONINSTITUTIONAL

There is a conscious attempt not to institutionalize the new ministries. They are simply organized to meet needs that may exist for a short time. When the needs no longer exist, the ministries will change. If they become institutionalized, change is more difficult to achieve.

RANGE OF THEOLOGY

Most of the new youth ministries have a strong theological base. They have developed as new forms primarily because those involved in them have strong beliefs and a commitment to these beliefs that lead them beyond present structures.

The theology of new youth ministries covers a wide spectrum of beliefs. Some youth ministers would classify themselves as conservatives, some as liberals, some as humanists. But certain theological perspectives seem to be held in common.

The new youth ministries embrace an existential view of the church. They are concerned with meeting human needs now, not preparing people for an ideal hereafter.

Many of the new youth ministries embrace a theology of hope. They believe that change can occur within their lifetime, that a new future can be foreseen on earth.

The new youth ministries take seriously an incarnational theology. They believe that God is at work in their lives and in the world around them, that He is constantly being reborn and that His work is accomplished through human sweat and toil.

THE NEW YOUTH MINISTER

In the past, the "youth minister type" was usually a young, attractive man (never woman) who was a good athlete, song leader, and comedian.

More recently, the description might be a young man with long hair who plays the guitar, is anti-Establishment, and wears army fatigues and boots.

However, it would be very difficult to stereotype any of the youth ministers involved in the ministries described in this book. There are radicals, revolutionaries, and conservatives. There are also scholars, artists, and educators. There are men in their twenties and women in their fifties. There are men who dress in army fatigues and men who always wear a business suit.

But all of these people have a charisma that enables them to develop a significant ministry with youth. The charisma is not magical. They are simply open, accepting people who know who they are, and not afraid to share themselves with youth.

PLURALISM

Youth ministry today is not limited to a homogeneous group of youth within the church. It is ministry with straight suburban types, "freaky" long-hair types, ghetto kids, gang leaders, runaways, motorcycle gangs, delinquents, and the kids in "Middle America."

Different forms of ministry have been developed to deal with this wide range of youth population.

A church no longer needs to depend upon a single denominational program with step-by-step plans for ministering with the "average" white, middle-class, suburban youth. Now, a variety of models have sprung up in local areas for ministering with the great plurality of youth who exist in our culture.

YOUTH AND ADULTS MINISTERING TOGETHER

In many of the new youth ministries there is a conscious attempt to facilitate youth and adults ministering together. The program is no longer handed down from adults to youth. It is developed together, with both youth and adults bringing to it their own special contributions.

The Response to the Crisis

In addition, many of the new youth ministries have ministered to adults who are not directly related to the program by helping these adults understand and accept youth in their communities. The generation gap is a reality in most communities, and many of these ministries have tried to bridge this gap.

A New Process

Perhaps the most distinctive characteristic of the new youth ministries is the process through which they emerge. No longer is this process designed by denominational offices and provided in indexed three-ring binders. Instead, it emerges as a creative response to felt needs in a local situation.

The next chapter describes this process in detail.

CHAPTER 3

The Youth Ministry Process

New forms of youth ministry are unique responses to particular needs. Although there are some similarities between needs in different communities, it is rare that the same model is effective in more than one community, and ministers who have tried to duplicate a model from another community have met with disappointment. On the other hand, similar models have emerged in different communities and seem to be successful.

This leads to the conclusion that the process a group goes through in determining the shape its ministry should take is as important as the final product the group designs. And it is this process, rather than the product, that can be transferred from community to community.

An Emerging Design

Perhaps the one thing that needs to be said over and over about the process of new youth ministries is that it is based on an emerging design. Very simply, this means that the end is not in sight when a project is begun. Although the objective is very clear, the means of reaching this objective may be constantly revised throughout the life of the ministry.

To most persons involved in youth ministry, this is an entirely new way of working. We are accustomed to developing pro-

The Youth Ministry Process

grams around a set time schedule (Sunday morning and evening), a limited number of methods (recreation, study, work projects), and defined settings (the church school, youth fellowship).

But persons involved in new youth ministries have had to create their own structures, develop their own methods, design their own settings. It is an experimental process, and it is extremely frustrating. At the same time, however, it is extremely rewarding because it is creative, and this creativity keeps it alive. (Creativity is discussed more fully later in this chapter.)

While this book is an attempt to make the task of designing new youth ministries easier by describing how others have gone about it, it should not be seen as a manual with step-by-step plans. The concept of an emerging design is absolutely essential to new forms of ministry and anyone who attempts to completely duplicate another's experience will be disappointed.

Perhaps the most helpful thing we can do here is to review the planning process used by youth ministers in creating new ministries, pull together the elements with which most new ministries work, review the new skills that youth ministers have had to acquire, and describe the creative approach used in new ministries.

These things, put together with the characteristics of new youth ministries described in the previous chapter and the task of new youth ministries described in the first chapter, should enable you to create your own new forms from an emerging design.

The Planning Process

An emerging design does not diminish the importance of planning. If anything, it makes planning more important. Plans must constantly be made, tried, evaluated, and new plans designed. Planning is basically a problem-solving process, and involves the following steps.

CLARIFYING THE PROBLEM

Assuming that a need has become obvious (either through a crisis or through a job description), begin by asking questions that will help clarify the problem.

You may "ask around" about the problem: Interview youth and adults who are involved in it to find out all of its ramifications.

You may get at the need through observation: Walk the streets, have lunch at the school, sit in on some youth meetings. In this technique, you will have to take careful notes and discipline yourself to write up your observations so they can be applied to solving the problem. You might also have another person observe at the same time in order to validate your observations.

You can also conduct a survey, usually by using a written questionnaire. This is a technique that has been used and often abused a great deal in youth ministry. A questionnaire must be carefully designed in order to gather the information that is needed. When possible, a consultant should be brought in to develop a scientific data-gathering instrument.

ANALYZING THE PROBLEM

After sufficient information has been collected about the problem, it must be carefully analyzed. This is a crucial step.

In analyzing information, the important thing is to decide what is most significant. It is a process of narrowing down, of selecting the most important trends and reducing them to one or two important findings.

There is always a temptation to use information to verify an assumption that was made before the facts were collected. This can be avoided by having several people analyze the information or by bringing in an impartial outsider.

At any rate, the analysis should be as objective as possible. If the information has been carefully collected and the analysis is both precise and objective, the resulting program will probably meet the need it was intended to meet.

STATING AN OBJECTIVE

The objective of the program must be clearly stated early in the planning process. This will enable the program to be accurately interpreted. It will also help you secure funding and program resources, and will provide direction and focus for the resulting program.

The objective should be as specific as possible: not simply "Help the kids that hang out on High Street," but "Provide recreation for the kids on High Street" or "Enable High Street youth to discover problems of their community to which the church can respond."

DEVELOPING A PROGRAM

The program should be developed to meet the specific objective. It should be planned in as much detail as possible before it is initiated. Planners should know who is going to staff it, how much money will be needed, how long it is expected to run, what kind of facilities are needed, what kind of program resources will be used, how it will be publicized, and who will be directly responsible for it.

EVALUATION

Probably one of the most significant things that has happened in new youth ministries is the emphasis that has been placed on evaluation—and the willingness to drop a program that is no longer effective. For years, churches used programs verbatim from denominational headquarters. When the programs were dropped by the denominations—usually several years after they had actually become ineffective—churches expressed tremendous resistance to the proposed change to a new approach. But in new youth ministries one of the givens is that nothing lasts forever. When something is no longer alive, it should no longer exist.

Plans for evaluation should be made at the time a program is designed. The evaluation instruments should measure accurately how well the program is meeting its original objective, and whether this objective is still relevant.

Evaluation can take many forms. One youth minister has a staff meeting every week to evaluate the effectiveness of all the things the staff is involved in. Other groups set a time limit on their programs and evaluate them at the end of that time with questionnaires, interviews, and observation as evaluation instruments. In other groups evaluation is very informal; the group knows when something is dying and it simply works on a new idea to replace it.

The Elements of New Youth Ministries

The planning process takes shape around certain elements that seem to be common to the new youth ministries. Most of these have been a part of youth ministry in the past, but they have assumed a different form or added importance in youth ministry today.

As indicated earlier, these elements are put together in different ways to create different forms of ministry. But the same elements are present in nearly all the ministries covered in this book.

A BASE OF OPERATION

First, there must be a base of operation. Usually this is a church, but it might also be the community. Within this base there is a need for youth ministry. If all the needs of youth are being met in the church or in the community, there is no need for a youth ministry. But the opposite is usually true.

A SUPPORT COMMUNITY

A support community is vital in the new youth ministries. If the youth minister has been employed by a church, he needs to organize a committee or develop contact with a small group of people within this church who can be in on the youth ministry process from the beginning, have an investment in it, and provide him with needed support.

Of course, the youth with whom he is creating a ministry will provide some support. But because many new youth ministries become controversial, the wise youth minister brings in some adults early in the process who have power at policy-making levels and who can stand up with and for him when controversy develops.

STAFF

Most new youth ministries have a staff, either paid or volunteer. In the Second Congregational Church of Greenwich, Connecticut, the senior highs staff a junior high program and the junior highs staff an elementary program. Many new youth ministries use seminary or college students on a part-time, paid basis. The East End Community Ministries in Pittsburgh use VISTA Volunteers.

FUNDING

Funding is probably one of the most essential, yet most difficult elements of the new ministries to control. Unfortunately, most churches do not take youth ministry as seriously as they do the upkeep of their building. They allot only marginal funds to it; when it becomes controversial, even these marginal funds are withdrawn.

As a result, many youth ministers spend a great deal of time finding sources of funding. A large percentage of the ministries investigated for this book were using some government funds. Other funds came from individual contributions, foundations, and community sources—all of which must be solicited. Since funding agencies tend to exercise control over the projects they fund, the youth minister spends another large block of time interpreting what he is doing in order to receive continued financial support. (See Appendix C for information on securing foundation grants.)

SPACE

Today space does not always mean a room in the church. In fact, this is often an unsuitable option because many church members object to the use youth make of the church building. Creative youth ministers search for space in vacant stores, public buildings, and school facilities.

Almost no attempt is made to build structures for the new youth ministries. The needs of youth change so rapidly, and thus the programs change so rapidly, that most youth ministers do not want to be saddled with a building that may then dictate the kind of program they can develop.

PROGRAM RESOURCES

Program resources are vital to new youth ministries, and very few are being provided by national denominations. The youth minister must spend a portion of his time locating resources: people in his community, printed and audio-visual materials from various publishers, medical supplies for medical programs, food for free food programs, and so on.

Skills in New Youth Ministries

The elements described above are shaped into a youth ministry by persons we refer to as youth ministers. This term does not describe only professional clergy who work with youth. It also embraces adult volunteers and youth who are themselves engaged in ministry.

These youth ministers have had to develop new skills as they have developed new forms. Some of the most important of these skills, but by no means the only ones, are the following.

GROUP PROCESS SKILLS

Many persons involved in new youth ministries find that skill in group process is one of their most important tools. Group process has become a fairly sophisticated field, and many denominations offer opoortunities for developing skill in it.

The National Training Laboratories (NTL) offer some excellent group process labs. Universities offer courses in group process in schools of education. (Other training centers are listed in Appendix A.)

COMMUNITY ORGANIZING SKILLS

Skill in community organizing is particularly helpful in the types of youth ministry that offer direct services to youth. These skills include learning to organize local residents to help solve their own problems, learning to work with existing community organizations, and learning to develop indigenous leadership.

Many youth ministers have learned community organizing skills through trial and error on the job. However, some universities offer courses in community organization.

POLITICAL ACTION SKILLS

Political action skills are necessary in youth ministries that attempt to change political structures, such as schools. The church is just beginning to become involved in political action training. (Locations of church action training centers are given in Appendix B.)

The Creative Process

Today's youth ministers have used their new skills and the planning process to pull together the elements of youth ministry into forms that are relevant to a new generation. The process they have used can best be described as a creative process, not a step-by-step design. It is a style of working that characterizes their approach to the youth ministry task.

THE CREATIVE YOUTH MINISTER

The creative youth minister has many ideas. And he (or she) is flexible with these ideas. If one idea doesn't work, he scraps it and moves on to another. He doesn't become bogged down with one way of working out a problem. He takes many approaches and develops many different kinds of results.

The creative youth minister is open. He isn't boxed into a rigid theological position or a static image of youth. He allows new experiences to change his ideas and his beliefs. He learns from youth and with youth. He adapts to meet new situations as they arise.

The creative youth minister carries little "baggage." He doesn't have preconceived ideas about the way things ought to be. He isn't hung up about large youth groups or successful programs. He is interested in meeting needs in whatever way he can. And the resulting model is often quite unpredictable.

The creative youth minister is willing to take risks. He may never have tried a project before and funds may not yet be committed for it, but he moves ahead.

He does not copy what someone else has created, or pick up a program from his denominational headquarters and duplicate it in his own Sunday night group. He doesn't even have a Sunday night group unless there is a real need for it. He begins with the needs that exist in his own situation and develops a model that is uniquely his.

This is not to say that the youth minister cannot rely on denominational headquarters, the church in the next town, or even this book for ideas or direction. The basic elements in all youth ministry are the same. But the way these elements are put together will depend upon his own and his group's creativity.

The creative process in youth ministry is similar to the creative process in the arts. It is approaching a task with openness and versatility, experimenting with many ideas, and taking risks that may lead to failure or to new and creative forms.

THE PLACE OF INTUITION

One aspect of the creative process that is often overlooked in youth ministry is the role of intuition. Many creative youth ministers, as most artists, make many of their decisions by intuition. When all the facts are in, when all the information has been analyzed and needs determined, they know how to put the elements together into a creative whole. Their knowledge is intuitive. They can't always say why they feel it should happen this way. But is usually works.

Perhaps they have developed a feel for what works through years of experience. Perhaps they really do have creative genius. Or perhaps, as some would say, the Holy Spirit is at work.

At any rate, their intuition should be trusted, because the intuitive decision of the creative person is often the best decision—and it is almost always the most creative decision.

DANGERS IN THE CREATIVE PROCESS

There are some inherent dangers in using the creative process in youth ministry.

Ownership

Everyone is possessive of the thing he creates. He has given a part of himself to it and so it becomes an extension of himself. This can lead to the youth minister feeling that he "owns" a program he has created. He then becomes reluctant to have others tamper with it and especially reluctant to see it phased out.

However, a program is never owned by one person. Once it is shared, it becomes the property of the group it has been shared with, and they should have the privilege of deciding when it should be dropped or how it should be revised.

Creating as an End in Itself

Another danger is that persons will become so enamored with the process of creating that they will create something new when it is not needed, just for the sake of being involved in the creative process. Creative youth ministry must remain relevant. It must have well-defined goals and meet specific needs or it has no rationale for existence.

Manipulation

The creative youth minister must also face the temptation of manipulating youth to achieve his own objectives. He may begin to think of people as a sculptor thinks of clay: something to be used in the service of his creativity. One way to avoid this danger is to share responsibility for creation with other adults and with youth. Persons who are involved in the creating cannot be manipulated by the creator.

Developing New Forms: The Process Reviewed

It might be helpful, at this point, to review the process that has been used in creating new forms of youth ministry.

COMMITMENT TO A RELEVANT MINISTRY

You must first see the need for new forms of ministry. In some communities, the old forms are still meeting the needs for which they were designed. But in many communities, youth have become alienated from the church and new forms of ministry must be created in order to be relevant to their needs.

Commitment to this objective is essential before you begin creating new forms. Developing new forms because it is faddish is poor motivation and will not stand up under the controversy that usually develops around the creating of new structures.

DEVELOPING A PHILOSOPHICAL BASE

We have not spent a great deal of time in this book on the philosophical base of the new ministries because it has been elaborated in several good sources already. It is reviewed, however, in the first chapter.

This philosophy, it should be noted, is an emerging one, and youth ministers are constantly expanding it as they work out their own forms of ministry. We believe it is helpful, however, to begin with the three principles described in Chapter 1: Minister with, not to youth; define the Gospel in terms of today's realities; and understand and minister with youth in their cultural context.

EVALUATING ALTERNATIVES

Chapter 2 describes the types of new youth ministries that have emerged and their characteristics. Use this as a guide to the alternatives open to you as you create new forms. (Note, however, that these are not the only alternatives; they are simply ones that we have observed.)

Once you have decided upon a type of ministry that seems to fit your situation, you can refer to the case studies that make up the main portion of this book to see how someone else went about designing this form of ministry. Take special note of the problems that might be encountered.

Better yet, visit with some of the persons involved in the form of ministry you decide to use. A list of possible contacts is provided in Appendix D.

PLANNING

Using the planning procedure outlined in this chapter, plan specifically for your own local situation. This is not a simple process, and will take the bulk of your time, if it is thorough.

DEVELOPING SKILLS

As you create a new form of ministry, you may find that it is necessary to increase your skills in some area, such as in human relations or political action. Appendixes A and B list several training centers for skill development.

CREATING MINISTRY

Developing new forms of youth ministry is a creative process, as was pointed out in this chapter. After you have completed all of the groundwork above, you are ready to create!

The Challenge of New Forms of Ministry

The task of creating new forms of youth ministry is not easy. For all of the dramatic results given in the next section of the book, youth ministers can cite a number of dramatic failures. For every new form developed, there has often been friction with an old form that has left scars on everyone involved. For nearly every personal triumph, there has been personal trauma.

Creating new forms of ministry is challenging, risky, exciting, dangerous, and sometimes lonely. But it must be done if the church is to be relevant in today's world, and especially in today's youth culture.

The Ministries

CHAPTER 4

Camden Youth Ministry
Camden, New Jersey

The building on Fifth Street is a run-down Salvation Army hall. Its drab appearance is brightened a little by psychedelic paint on the door.

The Camden Youth Ministry of the Lutheran Church in America leases the building now. There is no sign outside to advertise this, but inside you know it's a youth scene.

A large hall takes up the first floor. A coffee house is held here every Friday night. Upstairs are living quarters, with several bedrooms off a long hall, a lounge, a kitchen, two bathrooms. An unbelievable amount of "junk" is piled in these rooms. A stringless guitar juts out of a doorless closet. Stacks of papers line the walls. Several pieces with art possibilities are stashed in corners. Some good collages are hung on the walls.

Seventeen people (more or less) live in these quarters. Most are kids who have run away from home or were kicked out. They're trying to "put it together" here in a communal living experience. Reverend Bob Oberkehr, an ordained pastor of the Lutheran Church in America, is helping them with their search.

Conflict of Cultures

Bob became involved with Camden youth while serving as pastor of the Epiphany Lutheran Church, a few blocks down the street from the Salvation Army building.

There were very few youth in the church. The congregation was primarily suburban older adults who had been members of the church for many years. But there were many youth in the area.

Bob moved among these youth and became deeply enmeshed in their culture. When they expressed a desire for a coffee house, he opened up the church basement.

The coffee house operated for nearly a year. Then, in the summer of 1969, a drama program was added. It was through the drama program that Bob first met Larry Nelson, a staff member of the Lutheran Church in America Commission on Youth Ministry, headquartered across the river in Philadelphia.

Bob talked with Larry about his idea for a drama program. It would be held in the chuch basement on weekdays at noon. People in Camden's nearby business district could come for lunch and a play. So Larry went to bat for Bob and got money for some basic equipment. The plays were an instant success. The Camden *Courier Post* hailed them as the only legitimate creative art that was being done anywhere in Camden.

Meanwhile, a youth community was beginning to develop at the church. And church members were beginning to raise objections to the way their building was being used. Larry explained why:

"The kids who decorated the basement of the church had taken these old pious Sunday school posters and made them into beautiful posters, just by changing a word or two. And they had written some stuff on the wall that the older members of the church thought was pornographic. I don't think it was, but it could have been interpreted that way. And then one kid was sleeping in the church. I guess Bob knew he was there. Without any big deal, he started sleeping on a cot in the church. Then he picked up a dog—a big, beautiful shaggy dog. One of the church ladies was leaped on by the dog and it could have injured her."

The youth ministry was hotly debated in a series of Wednesday night meetings. Youth who knew their "home" was being threatened asked to become members of the church so they could vote on the issue. About forty attended a series of classes with Bob to prepare for membership.

At a final Wednesday night meeting, the church voted not to accept the youth into membership. And the program at Epiphany died.

At this point Larry Nelson, who had attended the meeting, approached the LCA Board of American Missions and proposed that they create a new youth ministry project in Camden, with Bob as the director. The Board accepted the challenge and agreed to pay Bob's salary, and the rent for a building.

The Salvation Army was approached about a lease on their vacant building and, after what Bob says was "an incredible wait," the youth ministry moved in.

Forming a New Community

The transition to a new kind of ministry was not as smooth as many had hoped. Bob said one reason was that the kids needed the church structure as a context for their ministry. "It kind of says from the outside in so many ways that we must get together," he said. And "getting together" was the biggest problem in the new community.

Also, he said, "Over at the church we had homogeneity. Everything was love, peace, and joy. But over here, you can say love, peace and joy, but 'Wow, you're different than I am so I can't love you anymore.' "

Bob is responsible to an advisory board, made up of members

of the Board of American Missions and the New Jersey Synod of the Lutheran Church in America. He presented a job description to this board before the youth moved into their new quarters.

Bob proposed that they continue the coffee house and drop-in center. He also proposed a crisis telephone service and thought a live-in program was essential to operate the hot line.

The coffee house has had a rocky existence. The kids responsible for it didn't seem able to take much responsibility. If a band didn't show up, they seemed incapable of dealing with it. Bob let them live through this phase of irresponsibility, and then dealt with the problems that emerged.

The drop-in center also ran into problems. Bob said "All during the summer we went through these incredible hassles. Personal stuff. Like people were coming in and they were bouncing off and running away and coming back a week later. We also had a lot of hassles with neighborhood kids. There's a sense in which everybody here wants to use the place in one way or another but somebody who wants to use it in a different way is unacceptable."

But there were some signs of reconciliation. Kids from the suburban areas who hung with the program after it moved to the new building began to relate with kids in the neighborhood. Some of the people living in the building took truckloads of young children from the neighborhood down to the shore or to parks.

The "family" in the upstairs commune faced many problems, but they began to work through some of them. Bob said, "Inability to communicate is our greatest problem. Like, each of the kids we're dealing with is afraid to be himself. We're trying to help them see this. Then maybe we can try to provide some tools for them to get at who they are and what they want to do."

Bob has continued his pastoral relationship to his new congregation in the commune. "Sometimes I have to be father and sometimes I have to be one of them and sometimes I have to be disciplinarian."

On Sunday afternoons, Bob leads a worship experience for the commune. He usually begins it with a statement from Scripture and it goes from there. Sometimes there is art, sometimes just rapping. The group is accumulating songs that are important to them and that may be published by the Lutheran Church in America. Bob is also working out a transliteration of the New Testament. When he gets a chapter finished, he calls the kids together and reads it. They all offer their suggestions for revisions and it sometimes moves into a deep theological discussion.

In the fall of 1970, the Camden Youth Ministry received a grant of $22,500 from OEO for the development of a demonstration project in self-support through creative expression.

Building Community from Scratch

Bob has done a lot of thinking about the way the Camden Youth Ministry has evolved. He feels that the most significant learning for him has been the intense struggle a people must go through to build community.

He said, "We began with the proposition that we are free and that we have a setting here in which we can do pretty much whatever we want to do. And that is extremely difficult to deal with. I try not to tell people what to do . . . except when the place gets so incredibly messed up that I have to scream and holler.

"This has been pretty much the story with every commune or every community that I've had contact with, unless there's some kind of rigid compact that people enter into before they join—that bends people so much that it's a drag. Instead of bending people into an ideal community, we're going about it the other way and accepting the freedom and seeing how we can make this work."

Bob feels they are trying to form a Christian community that

Camden Youth Ministry

does just the opposite of most churches. Instead of letting people in if they fit the pattern, they're trying to develop a pattern that will fit everyone who wants in.

He said, "Our motto is: Be who you are . . . as hard as you can. We don't take people and reshape them. We're reaching for a living culture rather than a culture that's bound to destroy itself."

In Brief

BACKGROUND

• Epiphany Lutheran Church in Camden was composed primarily of older members. There were virtually no youth and no youth ministry.

• When Bob Oberkehr came to the church as pastor, he developed a ministry with area youth. This resulted in a coffee house in the church basement.

• The church voted not to be involved in youth ministry and not to accept the "coffee house youth" into membership in the church.

• Bob was appointed by the Board of American Missions of the Lutheran Church in America to develop a community youth ministry in Camden, separate from the church.

OBJECTIVE

• To develop a relevant community youth ministry in Camden.

STRATEGY

• A building was leased from the Salvation Army.
• A program was developed, under the supervision of an advisory board of members from the LCA Board of American Missions and the New Jersey synod.
• The commune was partially funded by an OEO grant.

Program

- The program consists of a commune, coffee house, hot line, and drop-in center.
- The commune is experimenting with self-support through creative expression.

Problems

- The program met with tremendous problems when apart from the church structure, primarily because it drew youth from different backgrounds who had difficulty getting along. Most of the problems were personal.
- There was some community opposition to the operation of the program, particularly the commune.

Results

- Youth in the community have had some of their needs met, particularly the need for a place to be together.
- Some homeless youth have found shelter; some have begun to form a community together.
- Some people in the church (especially the members of the project's advisory board, along with Bob Oberkehr) have begun to look at ways the church structure must change to meet the needs inherent in a new youth culture.

CHAPTER 5

Telegraph Avenue Ministry Berkeley, California

The boy at the door was about fourteen. His hair wasn't long. His face didn't look hardened from drugs. But his clothes were disheveled and he carried a bedroll.

"Heh, uh, where am I?"

"This is the Berkeley Runaway Center."

"Yeah, I saw your sign . . . but, uh, what is it?"

"A runaway center. What's on your mind?"

The boy opened up to Gene Horn, director of the Runaway Center. He was over a thousand miles from home, and hungry. Gene told him about the free food program. The boy left his bedroll and said he would be back later to decide what he was going to do.

Response to a Crisis

The Runaway Center is just one part of the Telegraph Avenue Ministry, a cooperative community program carried on primarily in Berkeley churches. It had its beginning in an incident on Telegraph Avenue in the summer of 1968.

Dr. Ray Jennings had just been called as pastor of the First Baptist Church of Berkeley. A middle-aged man who had served a college church in Kansas and a mission assignment in Japan, Ray Jennings saw the church as a challenge. Its membership was declining and many thought they had to become community-oriented.

"I found out that to some, community involvement meant belonging to the Rotary Club," Ray said. "But I was interested in much more."

He got much more. The week his family arrived, they wandered up to Telegraph Avenue, a block from the church, to take in the scene. They stood on the corner of Telegraph and Haste listening to some sidewalk speeches; suddenly the police arrived and they found themselves in the middle of a riot.

Ray said, "To me, as a newcomer, it was just unbelievable. It was a peaceful assembly and suddenly 300 police moved in and told them to break it up and the people who were holding the rally left and then the police had a confrontation with the people left on the street with tear gas and clubbing. Both of my sons got clubbed."

The Jennings found refuge in Cody's Book Store and began a friendship with the manager, Fred Cody, that has been one of the mainstays of the resulting program. They had to wait for three hours before it was safe to return to the church.

Ray is a man of action and he didn't like what he had seen. So he called the police to complain. They said, "Take your complaint to the city council." He did, as did several others.

That led to the development of the Telegraph Avenue Concerns Committee, a group appointed by the city council to find a solution to the problems that were emerging on Telegraph Avenue.

The committee was composed of heads of city departments, the chief of police, people from the fire department, social planning people, students, and "street people," along with two ministers: Ray Jennings and Dick York, minister of the Berkeley Free Church.

The committee generated a lot of ideas. One that was carried out was the renovation of Telegraph Avenue. The sidewalks were widened about six feet, parking was eliminated, and trees were planted.

But they couldn't shake loose any money or support for their program ideas, so Ray and some others went off on their own. They developed the Telegraph Avenue Summer Program, a comprehensive program of services and education.

Food Program

A food program was set up in an old public school donated by the Board of Education. (The school has since been torn down.) Also housed in the building were a variety of classes, art programs, and seminars.

However the building wasn't adequate for the food program. The kitchen was on the third floor and kids had to go up there for their food, then come down and eat out in the yard. So after a couple of weeks, the program was moved across the street to the basement of the First Baptist Church. In 1970, the program was managed entirely by the church.

The food program consisted of an evening meal each day, served free to from three to five hundred street people. The meal was simple but nutritious, and was planned with the help of the city health department's dietitian.

During the first year the program depended on contributions from individuals and churches for its support. And kids supplemented the basic diet by soliciting day-old lettuce and other food from local supermarkets. Costs ran about six cents a plate. In the summer of 1970, the program received some funds from the state department of education.

Some of the street people did a major portion of the actual work in the food program. They helped prepare and serve the meal and were as regular as paid employees. Some arrived at noon every day and waited to go to work.

When problems of any nature arose, impromptu meetings of "the people" were called. The necessity for participants to have a say in the programs was recognized from the beginning, and it is a principle that has been adhered to religiously in every aspect of the work on Telegraph Avenue.

This involvement had an element of risk, pain, and even humor. One youth who worked voluntarily about eight hours a day in the kitchen had the nickname "Satan," probably because he wore a pointed goatee. He would sometimes answer the church phone extension in the kitchen with "First Baptist Church, Satan speaking."

During the school year, a food program is carried on by the University Lutheran Church in Berkeley. It serves meals six days a week to about two hundred people and is trying to develop a community around the persons who drop in to eat.

Free Clinic

One of the original proposals of the Telegraph Avenue Concerns Committee was a health referral service. The Summer Program committee developed this with the help of the city health department. It was set up above an old bookstore on Telegraph Avenue. Before long, the space proved inadequate and it was moved to Sixth Street.

At this time, residents of the Black community reminded the health department that they had been promised a clinic. It was hoped that the Sixth Street location would serve both communities. But neither community responded.

So the Telegraph Avenue Program committee developed the Berkeley Free Clinic. Now housed in the basement of the Trinity United Methodist church, it offers emergency treatment, more intensive treatment, psychological counseling, and group therapy.

The rooms of the clinic look more like a coffee house than a doctor's office. The walls are painted with graffiti-like slogans and some fairly good art—all in bold colors. Other art is hung around the rooms. One painting depicts a Hell's Angels' confrontation in realistic detail: muscles are bulging and the blood is very red.

The clinic, like many of the program's facilities, is a drop-in center as well as a service facility. Notices of volunteer positions and coming events hang on a community bulletin board. Many kids drop in simply to rap.

The clinic is staffed with volunteer physicians, counselors, and nurses. About sixty to seventy patients are seen each day during most of the summer; somewhat fewer in the winter. A twenty-four-hour switchboard operates as part of the clinic's program, making referrals and setting up appointments. Counselors are on call for drug treatment and emergency crisis intervention.

The clinic is supported primarily by coins collected in tin cans on Telegraph Avenue and by churches in the area. A small grant was also received from the Regent's Community Service Fund of the University of California.

The clinic is now open throughout the entire year.

Housing Program

Providing "crash pads" for street people is a major problem on the Avenue. Many street people are runaways or older transients who don't have any money for conventional housing. The Free Church has endeavored to meet this need but has found it difficult to secure sufficient homes willing to take in long-haired youth.

During the summer of 1970, the police chief was able to get the race track to open up portions of their jockey quarters and a system of vouchers was worked out. Kids were sold vouchers for one dollar that were good for one night's lodging. If they didn't have the dollar, they were assigned jobs, such as policing the quarters.

Now a large house has been secured that sleeps thirty or forty kids a night. Churches in the area are being encouraged to give money to the program so that kids who don't have money can use the facilities.

This has also become an all-year facility.

Coffee House

The coffee house, held in the basement of the First Baptist Church, began as an idea of a couple of young adult members of the church. Ray Jennings urged the group to do some planning and fix up a place that would be attractive to the kids. But time was short, so the sponsors simply hung a sign outside the church and opened up the basement. They were mobbed the first night.

During the summer of 1970, the coffee house was run by two summer volunteers who were paid subsistence salaries by the American Baptist Home Mission Societies. During the school year (it, too, has gone beyond a summer program), a seminary student from nearby Berkeley Graduate Theological Union is hired to coordinate the program. Between fifty and eighty persons attend the coffee house each night.

Clay Ford and Gail Tegler supervised the coffee house during the summer of 1970. Clay said it was a fairly unstructured program. Once in a while films which were made by street people were shown. One night there was an "open mike night," when street people talked with merchants and clergy from the area. One night they sponsored a dance.

But most of the time kids came in, listened to records, played Ping-Pong, read, and once in a while played the piano.

"It was a one-to-one ministry," Clay said. "As they began to trust you and could see that you really cared, you could share your faith."

Coffee is served, along with cookies or cakes that are donated by members of the church. Kids sometimes heat soup and occasionally make their own cake from the supply of cake mixes stocked in the kitchen.

Telegraph Avenue Ministry

Clay said that when he first arrived as a second-year seminarian, he was under "persecution for being a Christian."

"Some of the kids thought I was a 'Jesus Freak,'" he said. Most street people are turned off by the Jesus Freaks who roam the Avenue with their Bibles and their street-corner sermons. "A lot of people have a distorted view of what Christianity is all about from them," Clay said.

There are a core of regulars at the coffee house all the time. Of these regulars, Clay said about 50 percent gave up drugs during the summer.

"It wasn't a big thing," he said. "They didn't talk about it. But there were ways of finding out."

Drugs are one of the big problems faced in the coffee house. Greg Bearce, a seminarian who works there during the winter, says you can usually smell marijuana and pass the word through someone you know that the place is liable to be closed down if it's used. But it's more difficult to spot the hard drugs. On "heavy" nights, persons are posted near the johns to spot people who might be using them as places to shoot up. But even then, the janitor finds the remains of mainlining attempts from time to time. Programs to identify and help these users are now being considered.

The coffee house is funded by contributions of churches in the area. Since much of the food is donated, the budget is about $25 to $30 a month. The salary of the student director during the winter ($100 a month for the school year), is taken from the church's unified budget and credited as mission giving.

During the winter, Greg said, the program changed a little from that in the summer. Three afternoons a week karate lessons are given to girls. They are subject to attacks on the Avenue and need to learn self-protection. (These are not a part of the coffee house, but use the coffee house facilities.)

Some kids bring in clay to model and material to make belts and vests. Some carve wooden figures.

Serious rap sessions are a frequent part of the fare at the coffee house. These develop spontaneously, sometimes involving participants in the Free Church, which uses First Baptist's facilities for board meetings and committee meetings, and at other times centering around "Street Christians" from the fundamentalist Christian World Liberation Front, who often drop in. The atmosphere of the coffee house lends itself well to this kind of open confrontation of differing kinds of Christian thought and theology.

An attempt is made to have at least two volunteers at the coffee house each night. Volunteers from the Presbyterian church take charge one night a week.

One of the most effective volunteers during the summer, according to Clay, was a seventy-five-year-old woman. "People were drawn to her. She was a person that radiated acceptance."

A regular volunteer in the coffee house and a prime mover in all of the community involvements of First Baptist has been Fred Keene, a graduate student in math at The University of California. In his mid-twenties, Fred joined the church in the fall of 1968 and his enthusiastic support for a local church community ministry soon won him election to the Diaconate of the church, where he serves as Chairman of Social Concerns and something of a bridge between younger and older elements in the congregation.

The coffee house has been a learning experience for Greg, who supervises it during the winter. "Just getting to rap has been something," he said. "At first I had a hangup with names. I'd come up and say, 'Well, what's your name?' and they'd say, 'Just friend . . . or brother . . . just call me brother.' They had no names as far as we were concerned. A lot of them have police records and they don't like the name that is on their record."

The value of the coffee house, Clay feels, has been to provide a possibility for meaningful relationships.

"I tried to make the love of God a reality to them," he said. "I tried to show them that life is more meaningful when you're able to love and give rather than play the tough bit. I really came to care about them. It became just agonizing in some cases—with the people I really cared about."

Telegraph Avenue Ministry

Runaway Center

The need for a runaway center was evident from the beginning of the Summer Program. California law states that anyone under the age of twenty-one must be under the direct supervision of a parent or a guardian. In the summer of 1970, police picked up anyone on the streets with a pack on their back. Some 1,200 were arrested and punished, rather than receiving the temporary care and counseling they needed.

The committee for the runaway center began their planning by going over to San Francisco to talk with Larry Beggs, who runs the successful Huckleberry House. Then they spent six months in further planning, finally opening the center in March 1970 in a basement office of the First Baptist Church.

Margo Horn was hired as the director of the center. She and her husband, Gene, had been involved in a similar program in Portland before coming to Berkeley, where her husband attends the seminary.

A year-round program, the center now has a volunteer staff that includes, in addition to professionals, undergraduate and graduate students from the university who are receiving course credit for their work.

The program provides three options for runaways: (1) it will help them return home; (2) it will get authorization for the center to be responsible for them and place them in foster homes; (3) it will assist them to remand themselves to juvenile court.

In addition, the center provides phone contact with parents, crisis intervention counseling, family counseling, and a new program of prerunaway counseling in cooperation with the junior and senior high schools of Berkeley.

Like the Free Clinic, the main room of the Runaway Center looks like a coffee house. Two walls are completely covered with posters. On one wall a bulletin board displays information about runaways that are being sought—by police and by parents. (One "wanted" poster described a girl who was to be admitted to a state hospital and her friend who was on daily medication. Both had run from what they thought was an intolerable situation.)

The biggest problem the center has faced has been funding. Ray Jennings says it is almost impossible to get foundation support for something like a runaway center, and the main thing the state is supporting at the present time is drug programs. The monthly budget is about $1,100, $900 of which goes for staff. In December 1970, the program was nearly $5,000 in debt. The director was working for part salary. But the church was determined to continue it; it was not going to let the center die.

In addition to financial problems, the center has received a great deal of harassment from the community. "People aren't sympathetic to the problems of runaways," Ray Jennings said. "They think that by having the center, we're encouraging kids to come here. They don't realize that the kid who is in an intolerable situation is going to run away anyway—and that he is not always going to go back, even if he is arrested. We're trying to help kids resolve their situations in a meaningful way."

Harassment has also come from the authorities. In one incident, Margo was threatened with arrest for "aiding and abetting juveniles." She took a "leave of absence," after which her husband took over as director. During the summer of 1970, they were both arrested for interfering with the police in another incident in which Margo had sought police assistance in removing two drunks from the center.

A Christian Presence

The Telegraph Avenue Ministry has exhibited the effect that a Christian presence can have in a volatile community situation.

Telegraph Avenue Ministry

"Our neighborhood is probably one of the most evangelized in the world," Ray Jennings said. "There are always people on the street corner witnessing and passing out tracts—not just Christians, but Buddhists and others.

"We're not trying to push something on them. We're just trying to indicate to them our concern. The amazing thing to me is the number of young people—once that kind of relationship has been established and accepted—that turn to us for personal help and counseling. We do what we do, not to evangelize the young people but because our faith *requires* it."

The program has not attempted to bring street people into the churches. In most of the churches they would probably find a hard time fitting in. On the day we visited the Free Clinic a girl said to Ray Jennings, "Hey, do you have to go to church? Like, I started to come last Sunday, but I just had these things. . . ." and she looked down at her jeans.

Clay Ford feels, however, that a community of acceptance is the next thing that is needed in the program. "The situation on the street is very violent," he said. "So people are very cautious. They don't want to be too friendly to a stranger because he might be gay or he might be into hard drugs. And you don't know who's sick. It's all a kind of paranoia there. It's not fulfilling. But it's kind of exciting—in a perverted sense. There are always the drugs and the cheap sex. But after that, they really know it's a dead-end trip. The whole thing is a self-defeating kind of life-style.

"Some of the kids get off drugs and begin to establish meaningful relationships. I've seen it happen. But if they go back on the street, they just fall into it again. They need a place where they can become strong and give of themselves.

"The majority of the straight churches are dead. Christianity has become so lifeless and they have so many hangups about long hair that it just wouldn't work out for the street people to go there. Some of the churches are coming around, but it's taking them a while."

In the meantime, a few people from the churches are giving practically their lifeblood in becoming a Christian presence to a community of street people.

In the coffee house, white paper is regularly spread across the walls and paint provided so that the street people can express themselves in art and poetry. One youth lettered this prayer:

O Lord, I beseech you on this day to protect our young and smiling children, our trippers, who dance through our city never believing what pain awaits them at the hands of leechers. Protect our children, Lord, for they know not what life is. Amen.

The poignancy of that prayer from one who lives on the street is the incentive, the rationale, and the sustaining force of the ministry in Berkeley.

In Brief

BACKGROUND

- Telegraph Avenue in Berkeley had become a gathering place for runaways and other transient youth.
- Many of these youth had no access to medical services, educational facilities, counseling, housing, or food.
- Their presence had generated a great deal of hostility from the community.
- Relations with the police were bad, occasionally erupting into riots.
- Churches in the area had little or no appeal to youth and traditional ministries were not meeting the need.

OBJECTIVES

- To provide street youth with needed services and to enable them to develop and participate in providing these services.
- To improve community relations with street people.

Telegraph Avenue Ministry

- To develop a new image of the church as an agency of concern.
- To build a strong community ministry on a local congregational base.

STRATEGY

- A committee was appointed by the city council to study the problem and develop a program.
- When funds were not available for implementing the proposed program, a committee of private citizens, many from local churches, took over the concern.
- Facilities were secured in public buildings and in churches.
- Both paid and volunteer staff were recruited.
- Funding was done in a variety of ways. A small amount came from city and state funds, but the major funding came from church and individual contributions.
- Members in one church began to take action in crisis situations and concerned members of other churches responded.

PROGRAM

- The program consists of a free food program, a free clinic, housing, a coffee house, and a runaway center.
- Each program is run as a separate entity, with some coordination through overlapping personnel.

PROBLEMS

- Most programs, particularly the runaway center, have had financial problems. It is a controversial project and has not received overwhelming public support, which has resulted in a lack of financial support.
- Drugs have been a problem, particularly in the coffee house.
- Police relations have been tenuous at best.

RESULTS

- Youth have received needed services and have involved themselves in the programs.
- The community has been made aware of the need to respond to the presence of transient youth.
- Meaningful relationships have been established with some youth.
- Opportunities have been provided for volunteers to be involved in meaningful service and to understand the Berkeley street culture.
- The churches in the area are gradually acquiring a new image of youth.

CHAPTER 6

The Community
Oberlin, Ohio

Oberlin, Ohio (population 9,000), looks like a small New England town transplanted into the Midwest. There is a large town square, with the colonial structure of the First Church (United Church of Christ) on one side and the buildings of Oberlin College on another. It all looks very ordered and very proper.

The calm appearance is maintained at any cost. In the late sixties, student activism on the Oberlin campus created a small flurry of excitement. Black unrest (the town is 30 percent Black) added fuel to the fire. But the sparks were quicly extinguished by repressive legal tactics. Youth mouthed their parents' clichés about outside agitators and radicals and settled back into apathy.

Training for Action

Their apathy was jarred in 1969 when some youth from First Church attended a conference during Thanksgiving vacation. The conference was sponsored by area churches in cooperation with the Division of Christian Education of the United Church Board for Homeland Ministries. Reverend Bob Burt, of the national staff, had contacted Reverend Don Spencer, associate minister of Oberlin's First Church, along with several other area pastors and arranged for the conference to be held in order to help youth become involved in political action in their local communities.

Ten youth from First Church attended the conference. They met with other area youth and a team from Concerned Youth (an ecumenical political action group from Rochester, New York). They talked about political issues in their community and learned some practical skills for effecting political change.

Their training had several components. First, youth were taught how to view their community, especially the interaction among the people living there. Then they were trained in research procedures, so that they could operate from a sound base of facts. There was training in developing proposals and in the ways community patterns can be changed.

Phase I: The School Library

The Oberlin youth debated many community issues at the conference. They finally decided to attack the problem of book selection for their school library. Many books that they thought were both educational and politically relevant were never placed in their library. (One example was *The The Autobiography of Malcolm X.*)

The group returned home with some new skills and a strategy. They developed a list of books they thought should be on the shelves of the school library. They prepared statements about their concern that were read from two local church pulpits. They collected funds from church congregations to purchase the books and drafted a press release.

When the books had been purchased, the group presented them to the school. After referral to the school board, all but two were accepted, a month after their presentation.

Group Tension

The group was successful in their first venture into the arena of political action. But they left part of their group behind. The members of the Fellowship who had not attended the November conference felt left out. So a retreat was held during Christmas vacation to bring the rest of the group into the fold.

It was a difficult task. Some youth were receiving parental pressure not to become involved in political action. (One boy said, "My parents didn't tell me what to do, but they hoped I would drop out.") Other youth felt they wanted other things from the church, such as a chance for personal growth and study that was not action-oriented.

So the retreat that was planned to train the rest of the group in political action developed into a search for the direction the Fellowship would take. Two task forces were formed: one to develop programs for Sunday evenings and the other to develop a strategy for more political action.

Phase II: Independent Study Proposal

The action task force chose the school curriculum as their next focus and developed a proposal for an independent study program. This was an attempt to permit thirty students the option of studying one particular social or political problem rather than take courses in English or social studies. The study would embrace content usually taught in English and social studies, but it would integrate this content into a meaningful whole.

The problem proposed for the initial program was:

Assuming that our country is in the midst of a political and social upheaval, we would wish to investigate the historical and social basis for this movement. We want to come to know if there is any validity in the theory that America is about to undergo a fall that is analogous to the fall of the Roman Empire. We want to compare our "Renaissance" to the first Renaissance. We want to know if our rebellions are merely products of the so-called Hegelian-dialectic theory or are they valid and progressive.

The proposal was very carefully worked out. It included provision for class time, research time, faculty teacher-advisers, evaluation, credits, and parental approval.

The independent study program proposal was submitted to the school board in January and accepted. Again, the group had met with success in attempting to change structures. (However, the program was not implemented until the following January, due to a change in administration.)

End of the Fellowship

At about this time, five youth traveled to Rochester for an observation-evaluation weekend with Concerned Youth, the group that had handled their original training in November. They returned with a determination to confront the entire Fellowship with the need for action.

After their confrontation, intense conflict developed in the Fellowship between those who wanted a personal-growth-oriented fellowship and those who wanted political action. A day-long conference was held, ending with the death of the Fellowship.

Throughout February and March, the action group continued to try to bring about social change. They set up a draft-counseling center. They challenged the school's choice of an American Indian as a mascot. They began publishing an underground newspaper, *Splinter*.

Many of these efforts were successful, but they were carried out by individuals and small groups rather than by the whole group, and they were not always well planed or sufficiently

The Community

evaluated. The group felt that it was going off in many directions and lacked purpose.

Touch-In

In April, three staff members of Concerned Youth came to Oberlin for a consultation. They helped the group see that they needed to have more purpose and to set priorities. Task forces were set up to help the group arrive at a goal and a workable structure.

Seven weeks were spent in developing a constitution for the group, which now called itself "The Community." It was tedious work, but it drew the group together. One girl said, "After spending so many hours in meetings together getting things worked out, we really were a group."

The constitution is an eight-page, single-spaced document that covers any possible structural problem. Called "The Community—Decisions and Style," it has sections on goal stance, power and decision-making, relationship to institutions, relationship to the institutional church, relationship to the minister of education, group discipline, leadership, recruitment, communities outside of Oberlin, relationship to *Splinter*, funding, wider adult community of Oberlin, study, and celebration.

The goals were carefully formulated:

We, as concerned people, are distressed with the present condition of the world, with the starvation, killing, overcrowding, pollution, racism, and hypocrisy. A multitude of problems afflict mankind, destroy his freedoms and his potential as a human being.

We feel that the majority of these problems are the results of repressive economic and political systems presently existing. . . . We see the basic conflict, both here and in . . . other societies, as being between human and inhuman values. . . .

We therefore dedicate ourselves to this goal: The establishment of a world community preserving the natural human dignity of man and devoted to the ideals of freedom, justice, equality, and love.

Confronting the Church

In creating the constitution, The Community asked serious questions about their relationship to the church. They asked Don Spencer to prepare some study sessions on the biblical understandings of community in the Old and New Testaments. After a great deal of debate, they affirmed their relationship to the church with this statement: "Our goal has its roots in the Judeo-Christian concept of community and the rights of man. This tradition is what we hold in common with the church. We are connected with the church because of our common roots and traditions and there are many different legitimate ways of expressing that tradition."

They went on to say that they considered The Community to be an autonomous structure within the church that was not subject to "control by the governing bodies of the church."

In June, The Community approached the Executive Council of the church, asking it to accept them, their goal, and their organizational structure and, upon acceptance, to provide them with certain tangible things: an abandoned office, office equipment, staff (minister of education) and facilities.

The Executive Council could not agree about accepting The Community. They tabled the proposal so that the group's document could be rewritten.

The Community met in caucus and prepared the following statement: "We feel the document is at a proper level of clarity from which to operate. We feel that the language of our document best expresses our style and future intentions. We feel an urgent need to act. Therefore, we disassociate ourselves from the First Church. We would welcome further communications upon this matter from any concerned persons of First Church."

The Executive Council held another meeting a few days later and accepted The Community on the terms they had proposed.

Phase III: Disciplinary Action

The next fall, two youth groups began functioning at First Church. The Fellowship had been revived and The Community continued to function. They worked at different goals, with little communication between them, except that some youth maintained membership in both. This seemed to be the only way the youth ministry could serve the spectrum of youth involved in the church.

The Community began working on a new proposal. This one dealt with the process for disciplinary action at the high school, which they felt denied students their basic rights. They developed a document that listed their grievances: "That the student has no right of rebuttal, defense or acquittal" when he was charged with such things as truancy or disobeying school rules.

They said, "Our goal is to abolish the ruling that a student is suspended for truancy or skipping a class successively. Student council or the students will write the alternative to this ruling."

The proposal was turned over to the student council for action. By January 1971, no action had been taken, and The Community was beginning to suffer low morale.

A member said, "We had fellowship in our group last year, but this year there has been very little." The membership had dropped from twelve to six. They seemed to be unable to recruit new members. One member said, "I just wish we could get more people working on this kind of thing. Then we could do more."

At the same time, however, some positive things were happening in the church. In November, the Diaconate held a special meeting in which they asked the governing body of the church to appoint a commission to investigate The Community. But at the annual meeting, an adult nominated a member of The Community (who was also a church member) to the Board of Deacons and he was elected. The nominating speaker said he was offering this name because "if the deacons were going to investigate the youth ministry, it would be good to have a young person on the Board of Deacons."

Changing Institutions and People

The Community was able to bring about real institutional change in a city that tended to repress attempts at change. They accomplished this because they understood the method for effecting change and because they were committed to this goal.

But perhaps even more significant is the change The Community brought about in some of its members. All of the members spoke of having a greater sense of their own worth and their ability to do something about the world they live in.

One girl said, "I've changed incredibly. I had no idea how to change things. I just complained. I don't think I even thought about change. But now I know it can happen."

The group also changed the church's concept of youth and of youth ministry. They exerted their own power as a group of responsible persons who were calling the church to action. The church came to respect and support them.

In Brief

BACKGROUND
- Youth in First Church reflected the apathy of their community and seemed unable to bring about social change.

OBJECTIVE
- To enable youth to bring about social change.

STRATEGY
- Youth attended a conference and learned methods for bringing about social change through political action.
- The Community practiced the skills they had learned in several areas in their community.

The Community

• The Community struggled with its goals and developed its own constitution.

• They also struggled with their relationship to the church, and were accepted on their own terms, as an autonomous group within the church.

PROGRAM

• The Community developed programs for change in the following areas: book selection in the school library, independent study program for high school students, and disciplinary action at the high school.

• The Community maintained its group life through a program of study and celebration.

PROBLEMS

• The Fellowship group split over the question of whether they should be oriented toward personal growth or political action. Eventually two groups operated in the church.

• A number of adult members of the church were opposed to the goals and tactics of The Community. Open conflict developed.

RESULTS

• Youth in The Community were able to bring about tangible social change.

• Adult members in the church came to accept youth as full members of the church who were able to organize their own ministry.

CHAPTER 7

The Catacombs
Ventura, California

"The Avenue" is known. Mention it anywhere in Ventura, California, or the surrounding area and people respond with a knowing look. When parents can't find their teen-age sons and daughters, they connect the disappearance with The Avenue, and the often futile search begins along its pavements and back alleys.

Among the pizza huts and bars on Ventura Avenue is located the Bethel Baptist Church. Constructed some ten years ago by one congregation for its own parochial use, it was abandoned for lack of support. The Avenue did not respond to its churchly ministries.

After its first abandonment, it began its life in experimental ministry. A local congregation mistakenly assumed that the older people in the area would like to have a church of their own that was easy to get to. But it didn't work. The older people had no desire to be segregated from society while they worshiped. Finally, there was only a handful of older ladies left in the little green decaying building. Most pastors would not really consider such a church as a charge. Bethel Baptist was due for its second closing.

At about this same time, a young assistant minister serving in a neighboring community was having some difficulties of his own. Bob Rathbun had mixed a conservative theology with a strong social consciousness. His vision was not limited to the immediate desires of his own congregation.

Like many young assistants, one of Bob's responsibilities was to entertain and "keep interested" the youth of the church. The philosophy was to keep them happy and so keep them in the church. His ministry, however, began to include not only the young offspring of his parishioners but other youth as well. This added an element the church was not prepared to deal with. Different in appearance and deportment from the normal youth group constituency, the participants in this new ministry raised the fears of church parents for the contamination of their own children.

At this point, Bob realized that a ministry such as he envisioned could not be carried on through most churches. He needed a church that was down on its luck, some institution that had nothing to protect it. Bethel Baptist on The Avenue certainly fit that category.

In order for Bethel and Bob to come together, Bob had to enter a plea for a six-month extension to Bethel's life. The plan for a church for older people had bombed. For the older set, doing their own thing definitely did not include going to church with only the old folks. With money scarce and no chance for the church to become independent of denominational funding, the experiment was about over.

But Bob won his plea. He was given six months to see what could become of Bethel Church and The Avenue. The congregation consisted of twenty older ladies.

Finding a Place to Begin

The man and the place had now come together with a hope of ministry. But The Avenue was not going to break down any doors to be ministered to. The green church building remained as an incongruous part of the grubby scenery. Young people in need continued to walk by without seeing it.

Bob began to search for a way. He asked probation officers,

policemen, court judges, clergymen, and businessmen what they saw as the great need on The Avenue. The answer was a place where the kids could be without fear. A place where someone would listen, where they could talk to each other, where they could sleep in for the night if they needed to, where they could begin again to build on their own "creative" urges.

Ventura Avenue was not built on trust. Kids from all over the state came here to become engulfed in anonymity because they had lost trust. Anyone attempting a ministry of trust and acceptance would have no chance of being believed or even heard. Trust comes only from being trusted. Somehow Bob Rathbun had to find a way to show that he and Bethel Church were there to trust.

Juvenile court became his avenue of entry. Young people appearing before the court needed someone to stand for them. They needed someone who would make an honest attempt to understand their predicament from their point of view. It was no easy task for people reared in the shadow of law and order to stand on the side and in the place of people who violated their laws in the most flagrant ways. Bob Rathbun wanted to try and he watched the juvenile court for an opportunity.

Three boys appeared in court on charges comparable to assault and battery. Their case involved many brushes with the law but the present charge was the brutal mauling of a third boy. They faced juvenile detention. The mauling, however, was the result of a violation of their own code. The three boys had a female friend who was involved in prostitution, a common enough occurence on The Avenue. Disagreement developed in the party and the third boy, the victim, threatened to report the girl's prostitution to the authorities. The other boys threatened to teach their friend a lesson if he should ever carry out his threat. He did carry it out and they carried out their own threat.

Bob offered to stand for the boys. To know Bob Rathbun is to know that he was making no attempt to use them as a means of starting his own thing. While not accepting their philosophy, Bob actually did see the justice of their argument.

The Catacombs

It was this sincerity of purpose that made it possible for The Catacombs to begin. Trust was alive on The Avenue. A missing element was supplied. It took no gimmick, no publicity campaign to bring The Avenue to the back door of Bethel Church. While the programming that emerged was by no means usual, it is obvious that it arose only to fill needs already expressed.

The Back Room Philosophy

Life at The Catacombs centers around the back rooms of the church. True, there is a coffee house (from which comes the name Catacombs). There is a sanctuary newly decorated by the kids on The Avenue. There are improvisational drama groups; a photography group; a musical production, "Alley Alley Oxen Free"; an on-again—off-again beach ministry; and others. But the back rooms are where the action is. The action is still trust and it has grown from two boys (no longer with The Catacombs) and Bob.

By now the trust has become a group possession. A constantly changing core group of about eighty youth congregate at different times in these back rooms. These are not beautifully appointed quarters. Everything from the basement up has the marks of a twentieth-century junkyard. Most of the furnishings have been hauled in from the discard pile without any repair. On the walls are some excellent samples of photography and darkroom work. But the general appearance is clutter. To the denizens of The Catacombs, it is their own. In these quarters no one feels afraid to swing a leg over an overstuffed chair. If something breaks, who will care? It was most likely already broken.

In theory, the basement houses the coffee house and a lounge. The second floor is a general office and meeting room. The third floor, which can best be defined as a more refined clutter, is Bob's office. In actuality, all three floors are simply a place to be.

The Catacombs' real program is what happens to the people

who from time to time find themselves in these rooms. The building itself is incidental, but a necessary incidental. In these rooms people come to respect each other. They adopt what has become the basis of The Catacombs' philosophy: to share with others whatever I am; to accept whatever the others share with me.

The major outcrop of this philosophy is that kids alienated from many places through odd and antisocial behavior feel welcome among this group.

The participants in this ministry cannot be typed. They all share in common an earlier sense of alienation, but each from a different perspective. They wear their hair long and short. They are bearded and clean shaven. They are square and hip. They have jail records and are clean. They come out of poverty and affluence. They roam The Avenue and they live at home. Their conversations reflect the conglomerations they are.

But it works the other way as well. Bob Rathbun, for example, has said that it would be very phony for him to hold back from the kids who he is and what he is. If a part of him is a strong conviction of the relevance and personhood of Jesus Christ, then Bob makes no effort to conceal it. That, he believes, is what makes him what he is.

Bob Rathbun is the strong figure at The Catacombs. What he is has been personally experienced by most of the group. The result is that what motivates him has become the important and dominating stance of The Catacombs.

How It All Hangs Together

The resulting ministry is an extraordinary mixture of the conservative and the avant-garde. Whatever is needed for existence, whatever is relevant, whatever is genuine is saved for worship, for belief, and for action.

The core group, which is constantly mobile, sometimes makes decisions in happenstance get-togethers, sometimes in

The Catacombs

semiplanned meetings in the rear clutter. The decisions are related to what The Avenue needs and what they themselves need. Bob Rathbun is around to prompt and generate ideas. Once an approach is initiated, however, Bob says to the kids, "Carry on." It is a unique ability to be able to keep hands off the procrastination, and the blunderings, and the wildness that emerge. But hands off is a part of the trust. The groups within the groups then struggle with what they are trying to create. Mostly they are creating an inclusive togetherness that emanates to others on The Avenue.

A part of the group concerns itself with planning the coffee house program. This is their contact with The Avenue. It has become a place to be, a place where something is going on. Mostly what goes on is live entertainment and a lot of talk. Runaways make themselves known to other young persons they are conditioned to trust in The Catacombs.

The group is protective of its place. Such a conglomerate mixture of youth holds the possibility of a large explosion. But the reputation has grown, fostered by the group's own approach, that nothing blows in The Catacombs.

This trust has extended not only to the kids on the street but to the local law enforcement people as well. Probation officers ask to hold their probation meetings in the clutter.

There are times when some of the kids need a place to spend the night. With permission, they spend it on a couch in the back rooms.

On a given day, some parents will stop by looking for runaway teen-agers, a law officer will stop by to chat, some adults will drop in to help, there will be a pool game in the basement, a car will be torn down in the back yard. A person will call for help for someone who is in juvenile court, a group will be working out their own frustrations in an improvisational drama, and a lot of people will just stop by to be there.

One of the strangest turn of events at The Catacombs is the growing invitation list from the more straight churches. Always in search of sponsorship, and with a reputation spreading over Southern California, Catacombs Associated has developed a musical interpretation of its philosophy. The musical is a borrowing from many sources, sometimes too schmaltzy, but always a sincere rendition of the feelings of the group. The cast is a mixture of former and not-so-former drug addicts. It has some members to whom the group has become life and some who are new passers-by. But it is evident that all have been and are searchers for a spot of meaning in a meaningless world.

The theology they don't know they have is conservative, except for one item: inclusiveness. This is an inclusive group with no sustained thought of freezing out anyone for any reason. Yet churches whose doors could not be darkened by these same kids are inviting them to sing and tell about what has happened to them. The activities that take place in The Catacombs would certainly not be condoned by most of the people who want to hear about them.

The Catacombs and Adults

Before The Catacombs ever came to them, Bethel Baptist consisted of ladies mostly in their fifties and sixties. Maybe they had no real say about what happened, or maybe they knew there was no other life for the church. But whatever they thought, they stayed. A strangely warm relationship has grown up between them and the kids.

Traditionally, a pastor with such a charge is entrusted to hold hands and sip tea. If The Catacombs was to be, Bob Rathbun could not do that. But a need for a ministry with the ladies existed. Its solution appeared in the kids themselves, and its visible form was one boy who volunteered his service to visit the ladies. He was a kind of symbol of a developing cross-cultural enrichment. It is a pleasant experience to observe the mixing generations, life-styles, and dress in the rather traditional Wednesday evening Bible class.

Perhaps this could only happen in Bethel Baptist in Ventura,

The Catacombs

California. Bob believes this place and this time were right. The absence of middle-aged adults made the going easier. The older ladies were better able to live with the kids for they had less to lose in every way, and in the end, they gained.

In Brief

BACKGROUND
- Ventura Avenue had become the place for runaways and alienated people
- Bethel Baptist Church existed as a dying institution on The Avenue.
- A young pastor was seeking a place where he could minister to need without the shackles of affluent Christianity.

OBJECTIVE
- To build trust in the youth on The Avenue by offering to them a caring and trusting community.

STRATEGY
- Bob Rathbun offered trust to some youth in Juvenile Court by standing for them.
- The two youth and the pastor began together to build a group life.
- The group life was constantly built through spontaneous and planned experiences carried on by the youth themselves.

PROGRAM
- Small groups were formed around common interests for the purpose of building trust.
- The youth were encouraged to do their own programming.
- A coffee house was organized for the purpose of communication beyond the group.
- The group experiences were encouraged to spill over into the traditional forms of the already existing church.

PROBLEMS

- With a congregation of the very young and the very old, money is a constant problem.
- Traditional churches like to hear from The Catacombs' kids but would not want most of them around and will not support the work.
- A constantly changing constituency keeps the pastor on a twenty-four-hour-a-day schedule.
- Some people in the community do not understand what is going on.

RESULTS

- Alienated youth have found trust.
- Families have come to understand each other.
- Youth have learned to give themselves over to the constructive building of a group life.
- Law enforcement agencies have been helped to understand the problems of The Avenue.
- Some alienated older people have been given a new vision of life with meaning.
- Countless kids have found a creative rather than destructive use for life.

CHAPTER 8

Operation Bridge
Omaha, Nebraska

The name was chosen before Simon and Garfunkle's song hit the record scene, but "Bridge over Troubled Waters" is exactly what this service attempts to be.

Operation Bridge is a counseling service for teens in Omaha, Nebraska. It consists of an office on Pacific Street, close to the West Side High School, and a professional counselor, Gordon Helberg. The bridge is built by Gordon and the teen-agers he counsels. As Gordon said, "We're building bridges between youth and other forces: parents, the church, the law."

Down the street from the office of Operation Bridge, right next to West Side High, is the church where the counseling service had its start. The senior minister of the sprawling 1,200-member Countryside Briardale United Church of Christ is the Reverend Robert Alward. He explained that the need for a youth counseling service became evident in 1967.

At that time, suburban West Omaha was hit with a rash of vandalism and break-ins. Over 150 homes were vandalized. When the police rounded up the offenders, they discovered that there were a large number of youth and that they were from all kinds of backgrounds. Some were members of the Countryside Briardale church.

Mr. Alward preached what he called a "whomperoo type of sermon." He talked about the pressures on kids, the generation gap, the lack of services for suburban youth. At that time, many adults were not yet aware of these problems. Even the drug problem had not yet surfaced in Omaha.

The sermon was a "best seller." People requested copies and 5,000 were circulated. Then a group was formed to try to find some answers and the idea of a youth counseling service emerged.

Operation Bridge is Formed

A counseling service seemed like the most crucial need to most of the committee members. At that time, there were no services of this kind available anywhere in the suburban area.

Countryside Briardale put up the initial funds for the first year of operation, $15,000. But in order to make it a community project, they sought the sponsorship of Christ the King Roman Catholic Church, Temple Israel, and the East Nebraska Mental Health Association. The organization was incorporated and a Board of Directors was formed of representatives from all of these organizations.

An office was secured and a counselor was hired: Dennis Jackson, who had formerly been on the staff of the West Side High School. He remained with the project for nearly two years.

Operation Bridge opened its doors on July 1, 1968. By then, drugs had really become a part of the West Omaha scene and parents were beginning to worry about the "youth culture." But sponsors of the Bridge still thought they would face problems in getting a clientele. However, in a very short time, vast numbers of kids began utilizing the service. The word got around very quickly and the idea that such a need existed was reaffirmed.

Bridges Are Built

The Board of Directors saw the purpose of the Bridge as twofold: to counsel young people and to sensitize the community as a whole, and particularly the adult community, to many of the problems that young people have, as well as some of the things young people are saying about the nature of this world.

The counseling purpose was immediately and successfully fulfilled. But the directors were surprised at how receptive the community was to the second purpose. Many seemed to have been waiting to have someone attempt to build this bridge.

Dennis Jackson spoke to over three hundred groups in the city of Omaha, telling the story of the Bridge. The media was very helpful in publicizing the story. Soon it became evident that a fund-raising campaign could be launched in the community. The funding is now totally from community sources: individuals, service clubs, other churches, businesses.

The sensitivity to youth problems that developed as a result of telling the story of the Bridge also led to other developments. Several social service institutions established offices in the suburbs. And four or five groups were organized to work specifically on drugs.

A New Director

Dennis Jackson resigned in January 1970. Gordon Helberg, an ordained Methodist minister and accredited counselor, was hired in May. The Board of Directors, meanwhile, surveyed the services that were now being offered to West Omaha youth and developed a job description for Gordon that fit in with these existing services.

Mr. Alward said, "Our contention is that drugs may be one of the most visible parts of the problem young people have today. But if you're dealing with drugs only, you're dealing, probably, only symptomatically with the young person. He has all the fundamental problems about how he's going to manage to live in this world, how he's going to relate to an adult community, how he's going to find some values. So our charge to Gordon was that he shouldn't avoid drug counseling but that's not the only thing in our bag."

The Youth Bag

Gordon says that drug counseling has really been minimal. Some of the kids admit to using drugs and some say, "No. I'm not interested at all." But on the whole, they don't come to his office because they have a drug problem. In most cases, he believes, youth are afraid to go to adults when drug abuse reaches a problem point. They go to their peers who try to talk them through a bad trip or talk them in or out of using certain things.

"I want to be there when the kids are willing to talk about it," Gordon says. "At the same time, it hasn't been a big thrust."

During the summer of 1970, the greatest concern seemed to be running away from home. Gordon said, "They feel the pressures up to here, and they're not sure how to cope with them. So they talk to their friends and one or two others are willing to take off with them, so off they go. A lot of them leave the community entirely; others will stay within the community but not go home."

Some parents call Gordon when their child has run away. Gordon says they haven't been aware of what has been happening. They call and say, "What in the world do I do for my kid? How can I help him? What can I do?"

In addition, Gordon says, the parents have a lot of tensions themselves. When a kid leaves home they feel guilty. They are afraid they have not fulfilled their parental role.

One parent called Gordon the second day after their son had

Operation Bridge

left. Gordon promised to get in touch with them again. "I didn't hear anything more for three weeks," Gordon said. "I don't go out and hustle the kids. I'll go out to be where they are, but I don't go out and try to make contact and say, 'Hey, may I help you?'"

Then the boy's father called and said, "We're coming in." The boy was with them. It was an excellent session. The father admitted he had wanted to get out on his own when he was young. He said, "When I was sixteen, I went away and worked on a farm." So the family came to an agreement. The son could live outside the home for the next six weeks of the summer, as long as he checked in with his folks so they knew where he was.

"Things worked out for this kid," Gordon said. "He's living on his own, wandering in the parks and what have you. And he's brought maybe ten other kids in to see me."

Other problems youth bring to the Bridge are loneliness and hopelessness. Gordon said, "So many of the kids feel that they have no one in the adult world they can relate to. Authority is not the bag it once was. I think we have carefully taught our kids through the years to use their intellect. Suddenly when someone says 'I'm an authority and you've got to reckon with me,' they say, 'To hell with you. What's your justification for your authority?' The adult does not know how to cope with this kind of rebellion and so there's an alienation from the adult."

And the whole business of hope. One kid said, "Well, hell, I don't have any tomorrow. What kind of tomorrow do I have to face? Vietnam? That's hope?"

"My job," Gordon said, "is to help the kid focus on what he is—to try to rally some sort of goal. I always feel that setting goals is part of getting a job done."

To illustrate, he tells about a sixteen-year-old girl who came in. "I'm a tramp," she said. "I've been laid by so many guys . . . but now I'm feeling real strange about it."

"We started talking about it," Gordon said. "She wasn't satisfied with what she was. So I said, 'Well, what do you want to become?'"

At the next appointment, the girl said, "I've been practicing this whole idea of my being in charge. I can call the shots. Someone else doesn't have to call them for me."

"She found that she could be the decisive factor in her own life-style," Gordon said. "Just because a guy wants to put the make on her doesn't mean that she has to lay down."

An Enabler

Gordon sees the Bridge as a specialized service. It is not a total panacea for youth. It should, instead, act as an enabler in prompting the community to respond to the needs of youth.

An incident in the summer of 1970 brings this into focus. Omaha youth had taken over Memorial Park. They had chosen it as the place to congregate. And adult citizens were upset. They objected to the kids lolling on the grass, sometimes *smoking* grass, and throwing beer cans around. The mayor proposed that the park be patrolled and that it be closed after dark.

Some youth asked Gordon to argue their case before the city council. Gordon said, "This is the basis on which I'll go down. My work is Bridge work. I will not represent either faction, but I'll say, 'What role can I play in helping both sides hear each other instead of making noises at each other?' " So he was asked to moderate a panel of city officials and youth.

In considering the future of Operation Bridge, Mr. Alward sees this enabler role expanding. "From the very beginning," he said, "at least one of the concepts of Operation Bridge has been that there would be hosts of problems that we might point to and urge other organizations in the community to do something about. We would try to keep ourselves as free as possible to do the unique job of counseling—and do it well. We feel our particular role is to be the enabler to get other things happening, but we shouldn't do everything ourselves."

Gordon has several ideas about other services that might spring up in relation to the needs pointed out by Operation

Operation Bridge

Bridge. "I think there could be a network of agencies. For one thing, I think we need to have some expansion in terms of counseling. I think the kind of thing we've seen evident in this area is evident in other areas of the city as well. I think the Black community could well use a Black roving counselor. They have many agencies working there, but who do they have who is not tied to an institution? I think it is important to have someone who is not married to an institution."

Gordon also sees a need for a "halfway house" or "runaway house." Another group in the city is working on this. Operation Bridge will be on the referral list of this house, but it will not run it.

A Lutheran pastor in Omaha has an idea about using some land his church owns for a unique youth ministry. A medical student has an idea for serving youth through a "rap house," using the incorporation of Operation Bridge, but developing a separate agency.

All of these developments have come about because a church started the ball rolling with concern, backed by financial commitment, which resulted in a new expression of youth ministry: Operation Bridge.

In Brief

BACKGROUND

- Youth in West Omaha were engaging in violent destructive activity because they did not know how to deal with their personal frustrations.
- Adults had little understanding of the real needs that brought about this violent behavior.
- There were no youth-serving agencies in West Omaha.

OBJECTIVE

- To help youth deal with their frustrations and to help adults understand and respond to youth needs.

Strategy

- The minister of Countryside Briardale preached a sermon that drew attention to the problem.
- A committee was formed to find a solution.
- A counseling service was proposed that would relate to youth through counseling and that would play an interpretive role with adults.
- Community backing was secured by involving two other churches and a mental health association.
- An office was secured and a full-time counselor was engaged.
- Interpretation was achieved through the use of media and through the counselor's contacts with community groups.

Program

- A youth counseling service with a full-time counselor was instituted.
- Other youth-serving agencies were encouraged to develop through the example and interpretation program of Operation Bridge.

Problems

- There were very few problems. It was not a controversial form of ministry and the community seemed ready for such a service.

Results

- Youth have been helped to deal with their frustrations.
- Vandalism in the neighborhood has decreased.
- Adults have been made aware of youth needs and, in some cases, have responded to these needs.

CHAPTER 9

Provadenic
Cleveland, Ohio

Growing up in the affluent Cleveland suburb of Shaker Heights is growing up with all of the material comforts and spiritual impoverishments of the "successful" American way of life. Some youth from these upper-class homes become runaways, revolutionaries, and drug addicts. Others pattern their lives after the Establishment they are a part of and perpetuate the cycle.

The Reverend Jim Knauf, a minister on the staff of the First Baptist Church of Greater Cleveland, located in Shaker Heights, has struggled for years to help youth become agents of change in their culture. The youth fellowship was organized into task forces. The group worked in civil rights. They attempted to influence political structures. But nothing really caught fire to bring about significant change.

Then, at a retreat in the fall of 1965, several things seemed to fall into place. The group had become acquainted with problems in Nicaragua as they talked with Gus Parajon, a young medical student from Nicaragua who was a member of their church. The father of a boy in the group, Ralph Hingson, was director of Brother's Brother Foundation, which carries on mass immunization programs in Third World countries. The youth were looking for a significant project to become involved in, and out of their discussion came a proposal for "Provadenic."

Organizing the Project

Their original plan was to go to Nicaragua to help with a mass immunization program during the summer of 1966. When the idea was submitted to the finance committee of the church, however, they suggested that instead of setting up a one-shot project that would cost approximately $10,000, the project should be smaller and be carried on annually.

The final proposal to the congregation listed their purposes as the following:

1. To provide on a continual and growing basis an opportunity for training our young people as leaders of today's church, and encouraging them to think in terms of Christian service in their vocations.
2. To motivate our young people for involvement now in the needs of the community and to provide an on-going training program for community involvement.
3. To involve our young people actively in the world mission of the church by participating in the needs of others and applying the doctrine of love in a positive work experience.
4. To participate actively in the missionary program of the American Baptist Convention.
5. To share with the congregation upon their return from such a project the rich and varied experiences gained from such missionary involvement.

There were some questions about going "way down there" when needs in Cleveland were so pressing. But the youth saw this as an extension of their local mission concern. Youth who were accepted in Provadenic were required to have had prior involvement in the church, in volunteer services, in locally sponsored work projects, and in Cleveland's inner city.

1966: Mass Immunization Program

Thirteen volunteers were accepted in the first year of Provadenic. The project consisted of a three-week mass immunization program in three "departments" of Nicaragua in cooperation with Brother's Brother Foundation.

The experience was an eye-opening one for all the participants in Provadenic. Many had never seen the malnutrition, disease, illiteracy, squalor, exploitation, and oppression of the Third World.

Dr. George Jackson said, "Going to Nicaragua, one cannot travel down a street without seeing what lies to either side of it. Poverty isn't hidden, like it is here in America. Your eyes are opened not only to the conditions that exist there, but you suddenly realize that the same conditions exist about you in your own country."

While in Nicaragua, some of the youth and adults became acquainted with the work of the IAN *(Instituto Agrario de Nicaragua)*. The Institute had purchased land from large landowners and had been given some land by the government. The land was divided into small farms that were sold for very little to poor farmers. The Institute had so established approximately twenty-one colonies with close to 5,000 farmers and their families living on them.

The group became concerned about the needs of the *colonos* and decided to return the next summer to work with them.

During the winter of 1967, Jim Knauf and Gus Parajon visited several of the colonies, selecting the General Somoza colony to work in during the summer. It was a very isolated, rural colony, far from any medical care. And the people were very friendly. They also seemed interested in helping themselves.

1967 and 1968: Public Health Program in Somoza

Because the scope of the program was enlarged in 1967, the First Baptist Church invited other churches to join them in sponsorship. The Garfield Memorial Methodist Church in Cleveland became an integral part of the program. Earlier, several other agencies had become related to Provadenic: the Nicaraguan Baptist Convention, the First Baptist Church of Managua, the Baptist Hospital in Managua, and the *Instituto Agrario de Nicaragua*.

The enthusiasm of the volunteers who had been involved in the 1966 project spread through the congregation at First Baptist and through the hospital where Gus Parajon worked. There was no need for recruitment; people were asking to be involved.

One person who joined Provadenic in 1967 said he didn't realize what he was getting into. George Jackson was a medical student working under Gus Parajon at the Cleveland Metropolitan General Hospital. He had planned to take part of his training in England and spend some additional time touring Europe. One day Dr. Parajon asked him if he would like to go to Nicaragua. He thought his way would be paid and jumped at the chance to see another part of the world without having to cut into his meager medical student's funds. He soon discovered, however, that his way would not be paid. In fact, he would have to pay around $400 to go. (Most participants paid their own way.) But he felt he was too deeply involved to back out. Since then, he has gone back each summer.

When the Provadenic group arrived at General Somoza colony, they discovered an area near the Pacific coast of Nicaragua with a population of 1,371. It was a collection of 209 fifteen-acre farms where corn and occasionally cotton were grown.

The *colonos* were just one notch up from subsistance farmers. They lived in thatch huts and had no provision for sewage disposal. Infectious diseases were rampant.

The Provadenic youth and adults set up camp in a schoolhouse and organized a clinic on the porch. Medical personnel examined patients, prescribed treatment, and gave shots. Meanwhile, some of the high school youth visited the *colonos* in their homes to find out how they could help. They assisted some in building latrines.

Dr. Jackson encouraged some of the *colonos* to build a clinic building. They were able to use it in the summer of 1968. Dr. Parajon described what working in the clinic was like that summer:

"There would be sixty people milling around when we opened. The temperature was ninety-five to one hundred degrees. Bill Cumming (a doctor from First Baptist) would see one hundred to one hundred twenty patients in an afternoon, in his small cubicle in the clinic. George Jackson worked in another cubicle and I in still another one. A sheet provided the fourth wall of each cubicle.

"As the patients came out, they were directed to the pharmacy, which was manned by two of the six nurses who had come from Cleveland. (Many of the drugs had been donated by pharmaceutical houses in the States.) We worked until six P.M., when it was pitch black. The last patients were seen by the light of a Sears generator—the only source of electricity for miles around."

After the clinic closed, the people milled around the central area, where the schoolhouse, cooperative store, and clinic were located. They talked with the high school students who had become their friends. On two nights a week movies were shown, usually relating to public health. One, in Spanish, used Walt Disney cartoons to portray the life cycle of the common parasites and their transmission, prevention, and cure.

During 1968, a survey was taken of the health needs of the colony. Cultures were taken from wells, and out of twenty, eighteen were contaminated. Children had died from diarrhea, tetanus, parasites, malaria, and whooping cough. By the time mothers had reached the age of thirty, they had had an average of 10.7 pregnancies. However, most of the families had only from five to eight children living.

The Provadenic team became concerned about their one-shot approach to public health. They were convinced that services should be provided on a year-round basis. Dr. Jackson gathered the community leaders together and after several sessions, they elected a Clinic Committee. The committee decided to charge a small fee for every patient visit and use the money to buy medicine and supplies. They contacted the Ministry of Health, which supported the program and provided antituberculous drugs, powdered milk, and a public health nurse once a week, throughout the year.

The committee also took over the latrine program, and by the end of the summer, thirty-five more latrines had been started.

In the fall of 1968, Dr. Parajon returned permanently to Nicaragua to work in the Baptist Hospital. He offered to come out to the colony every other Tuesday to help with the clinic.

1969: Community Organization

Provadenic was carefully evaluated each year. At the end of the 1968 trip, the group thought seriously about the long-range effects the program might have and decided that they needed to become involved in a literacy program, which would enable the *colonos* to better help themselves. They also decided that they needed to help the *colonos* organize themselves into a more effective community.

During 1969, college students from the First Baptist Church of Managua and nurses from the Baptist Hospital in Managua became part of Provadenic.

In the first week of the 1969 project, three clinics were organized: a general medical clinic (which treated 600 *campesinos*), a maternal and infant clinic (which examined and treated 437 children), and a dental clinic (which treated 93 persons).

Surveys were conducted to determine specific nutritional needs. A study was made of family planning. Wells were examined and families with contaminated wells were encouraged to chlorinate them or construct new ones. Instructions for building more stable latrines were given (only sixty built the year before were still functioning). A survey of colony roads was made. A bridge was repaired and an application submitted to CARE for funds to construct a culvert.

Literacy classes, using the Alfalit method, were started to combat the 70 percent illiteracy rate in the colony. One hundred and twelve women were enrolled in sewing classes. A pilot crop of peanuts (with the high protein needed in the diets of the *colonos*) was planted. And a community center was completed.

The program had moved from "We'll help you" to "We'll help you help yourselves."

1970: The Program Expands

Between the summers of 1969 and 1970, Dr. Parajon had organized a very effective Nicaraguan counterpart of Provadenic, made up of youth and medical students from Managua. They had worked in the clinic at Somoza and had come to know the needs of other surrounding colonies. The project at Somoza was almost self-sustaining.

So, during the summer of 1970, Cleveland youth and adults split into four teams and worked with Nicaraguan youth and adults in four colonies: General Somoza Colony, San José de Tonalá Colony, Israel Colony, and Puerto Morazan.

Helen Stciak, a nurse who had been with Provadenic for several years, told about the change she found: "For the first three years, no Nicaraguans helped, or very few did. Last year a lot came and looked from the side lines but they didn't do very much. This year they came and handled their own reading programs by themselves and we kind of got in their way."

Dr. George Jackson told how one *colono* from Somoza grew:

"Juan showed himself as a potential leader when we first arrived. He always tried to do what he felt would benefit himself and his family's health. He built a latrine the first year we were there. He built a new house with walls the second year we were there. And then when we started the literacy project, he was one of our most faithful students. After six months of studying, starting from the point where he could not read or write his own name, Juan was able to read at a sixth-grade level. He made all the signs for the clinic last year. He is probably reading on a seventh- or eighth-grade level now and he is becoming the major promoter of the literacy program, organizing committees, soliciting teachers, and so forth."

Some of the people in the General Somoza Colony were disappointed that the whole group of thirty to thirty-five youth and adults did not return to their colony in 1970. They had come to look forward to the summer excitement of so many visitors and had made fast friendships with some of the Provadenic regulars.

But other colonies had needs similar to those in Somoza, so the group split itself into smaller units to meet these needs.

A Cross-Cultural Experience

Jim Knauf has spent a lot of time thinking about Provadenic. One of his major responsibilities at First Baptist is youth ministry and he wants to be sure that the project is a vital part of this ministry.

Jim has seen tremendous growth in youth who have been involved in Provadenic. Some have even changed career plans. All have been faced with questions about their place in a world community and about their role as Christians who talk a lot about "caring" but often do not express it.

Jim feels that one of the most helpful results of the experience is the development of skills for influencing change. In the Provadenic experience, youth are involved in theologizing

Provadenic

(relating their faith to the situation in which they find themselves), analyzing (examining a culture with a view to understanding its problems and positions), and strategizing (planning, carrying out, and evaluating appropriate action to change the situation).

These skills can be carried over into involvement in Cleveland or in other places the Provadenic participants find themselves—and many have done so. Youth have learned and practiced these skills in a real situation. They know they can effect change.

Perhaps the meaning of the project can best be summed up by this poem written by Jansen String, a 1970 participant in Provadenic:

Cry naked baby
Cry, Cry, Cry
The world will feed you or drown with your tears
Cry naked baby
Bug bitten, bleeding, bloated and abused
Smelling of chicken and scrawny dog
Unbathed, fly infected
Dust baked baby
Succumbed of pig sweat
Sticky sewage
On your warted, callous baby body
Cry because you're dirty and diseased
Abandoned and fearfully alone
Sickly sad
And you don't know why.
Cry because you never had a choice
And never will.
Cry baby, holler, scream bloody hell
The world can't ignore you.
Cry baby, make us clean you
Make us feed you
Make us clean up the mess
The rich leave for the poor to wallow in
Make us remember

We too are children
Like you born by nature to the world
Unlike you, luckily born in comfort
Comfort we deserve as little as you deserve discomfort.
Cry baby, cry.
For the sorrow men of disinterest, self-interest make for us all.
Make us keep you brother in the family
In this world, our home
Make us see
We can't keep you alone in the germy, wet, rat basement.
Make us love you baby brother, not neglect you.
Make us realize how lucky we are
Make us see how like you we are
How we can never be free til your eyes are dry
Cry naked baby,
Cry, cry, cry.

In Brief

BACKGROUND

• Youth in the First Baptist Church in Cleveland needed to be involved in a major project in order to experience their own ability to bring about change.

• A doctor in the congregation opened the doors to involvement in a medical mission in Nicaragua.

OBJECTIVE

• To help youth in Cleveland become involved in social change.

• To meet the medical and community needs of Nicaraguans.

• To enable youth and adults in Nicaragua to be involved in social change.

STRATEGY

• A mass innoculation program was planned for the summer of 1966. It was organized in cooperation with the Brother's

Brother Foundation, which had similar programs in Third World countries.

- Youth and adults were recruited on the basis of their skills and former involvement in community projects.
- Funding was by individual contribution (most members paid their own way) and through the church budget.

PROGRAM

- In 1966, the program consisted of a mass inoculation program.
- In 1967 and 1968, the group concentrated on medical needs and public health education in one colony.
- In 1969, community organization and a literacy program were added.
- In 1970, projects similar to the one carried on in Somoza were carried out in other colonies.

PROBLEMS

- Problems were encountered in organization that would be present in any massive project of this nature: shipping delays in transportation of pharmaceuticals, breakdown in communications, and so forth.
- There were some personal conflicts that would also be expected in a project that involved close living arrangements.

RESULTS

- Youth grew in personal and social awareness.
- Some youth clarified career goals.
- Youth experienced their ability to bring about social change.
- Some intergenerational barriers were broken down as youth and adults worked side by side in another culture.
- Youth had an opportunity to "do theology."

CHAPTER 10

The Way
Quincy, Massachusetts

The storefront on East Squantum Street is in the middle of a block of run-down stores in a middle-class neighborhood of Quincy.

Inside the store, a long, narrow room serves as the meeting place, sanctuary, and "home" for a group of teen-agers who call themselves The Way.

The Beginning in Cambridge

The Way had its beginning in 1966 in Cambridge, where Gene Langevin was a student at the Harvard Divinity School. He had become interested in theology while studying at Harvard College several years before. His undergraduate thesis topic, "The Social Theory of Walter Rauschenbush," exposed him to the "social gospel" and he enrolled in Union Theological Seminary in New York. From there he went to Mansfield College, Oxford, England, and then back to Harvard.

While in New York, Gene worked with street gangs, involving them in wrestling and boxing clubs. In England, he visited delinquency prevention programs and worked in a home for delinquent youth. At Harvard, he was given a field assignment with the Boston City Mission Society, working with neighborhood youth in a struggling American Baptist Church in Cam-

The Way

bridge. (Gene is an American Baptist himself.)

Gene developed several programs at the church, which ministered to a total of six hundred youth, many of whom were members of delinquent gangs. Tension developed with the church, however, as people objected to boys smoking and using "bad language" in their building. Some youth were asked to leave and Gene left with them.

He sought another building for the program, but four churches turned him down for various reasons. The City Mission Society continued to back him, but he and his group found themselves out on the street.

A number of youth continued to meet with Gene at the Divinity School. He said, "We met there twice a week in the afternoon. At each session we had a little bit of general conversation and then I'd tell a Bible story and we'd talk about the Bible a little."

The group became fascinated with the story of the first church. They felt they had something in common with it. The first Christians had been thrown out of the church, persecuted by the police, and felt that nobody wanted them. The group identified with these original Christians and adopted their name, The Way.

They wanted to start their own church, but Gene was hesitant. He said, "I didn't want to start a new religion. But I thought maybe a new congregation would be in order. Maybe we did need a new structure to work with these kids." So a new congregation was formed and the group began developing their own liturgy.

One day Gene rewrote a popular song, using words that would convey Christian meanings. The group "dug it," so Gene tried his hand at a few more. Scriptural verses were put into street language by the group and contemporary prayers were developed. The group soon had a new service, and called it a rock 'n' roll service.

One of Gene's professors at the Divinity School heard about the service and asked the group to present it at an arts festival at Boston's Old South Church. Gene expected about forty people at the service; there were eleven hundred. The group danced to the rock 'n' roll hymns and photographs of this received international distribution.

Reaction, both positive and negative, came to Gene from all over. He was accused of "destroying Christianity" and of conducting "sexually oriented gymnastics." He received many tracts urging him to repent. But he also received much support and encouragement.

The group was given the offering of $120 for performing in the arts festival. They used the money to rent a vacant store in Cambridge for one month. They offered boxing and wrestling and a worship service once a week. Then, when the kids requested it, they added a second service in place of one of the nights of wrestling. A youth group from the Methodist Church in Winchester joined them for worship once a week.

Funds to keep the ministry going were solicited from area churches, but with no success. Gene kept the storefront open during the winter by paying the rent from his own pocket. When his own funds began to run out, he took a full-time job as a probation officer in Quincy and attended the Divinity School part-time. Hence the ministry was moved to Quincy.

A New Beginning in Quincy

The move to Quincy meant a new beginning in many ways. Some of the kids from Cambridge came to the new storefront on East Squantum Street. But the distance was too great for many to be deeply involved.

In Quincy, the neighborhood youth were not as organized in gangs as they had been in Cambridge. And they were younger. Some had been in trouble with the law. Some were probationers assigned to Gene by the court. Others were "long hairs." Most were boys.

The Way

More than forty youth became part of The Way and Gene needed help with the program. He approached the field work departments of two seminaries in Boston. Five seminarians from Boston University School of Theology and two from Andover-Newton Theological School were assigned to help him.

With the help of the seminarians, Gene developed a boys club program and several family clubs. The worship services were continued and expanded.

Rock 'N' Roll Worship

Worship at The Way has become highly liturgical, but the liturgy is relevant. Much of it is written by members of The Way.

The hymns are familiar pop songs with new words. A response to be sung after the reading of Scripture was set to the Song "Downtown": "Praise God for giving us this reading he gave us from his Holy Word. Amen." A new Gloria Patri is set to the tune of the Salem cigarette commercial.

Prayers and Scripture readings are put into contemporary language. One prayer goes: "Our Father, keep families from breaking up and the children from being sent away. Keep fathers from drinking too much and beating up on their kids. In the name of Jesus. Amen."

Two distinct liturgies have been developed: one for a rock 'n' roll dancing service and one for a rock 'n' roll communion service.

The rock 'n' roll dancing service is more informal than the communion service. It may last for three hours and includes two long periods of conversation and dancing. There are even refreshments. One person said, "It's like having a party with God."

The communion service lasts about an hour and a half. There is no dancing. Banners are hung and a table is covered with a white cloth to hold the bread and wine. Candles are lit. Hymns, prayers, and sermon proceed in quiet dignity. The communion elements are served by members of The Way.

Boys Clubs and Family Clubs

Because of the large number of boys that became a part of The Way in Quincy, the seminarians working with Gene organized a number of boys clubs that meet on weekday evenings.

The first part of the boys club meeting consists of informal recreation or projects. There is boxing, wrestling, and pool in the basement. The boys can read, listen to records, or create art. One group lined the basement walls with posters they made themselves.

In the middle of the evening, the members of the boys club come together for Bible study. It's not traditional Bible study. It's more like a rap session on the Bible and theology, tying it all in with what's happening in the boys' lives.

Family clubs are for boys who are in trouble with the law or with their parents. Each club has four or five boys and they literally become a family. They meet each week to talk over their problems and support each other.

If a boy is thinking of running away, he tells the boys in his family club about it first. One boy turned down a glue-sniffing party to attend his family club; he said, "I was thinking, maybe I could start a group like we have here. It would keep these boys from getting in trouble with glue-sniffing and things like that."

The family clubs also mete out punishment for members who need it. Gene feels that most of the boys need to be responsible to someone for their actions. Most do not have fathers in their homes and their mothers are unable or unwilling to discipline them. Group discipline from their peers fills the void.

Each boy's parent fills out a "progress sheet" weekly. It lists various areas in which the boy might have trouble: skipping school, being late to work, using alcohol, using drugs, missing a curfew. The boys bring these sheets to their family club meeting and talk about them with the other members. When punishment is indicated, the group talks it over and metes it out. It may range from washing the floors of The Way to a tighter curfew for the next week.

A Church for Teens

Gene provided most of the funds for operating The Way from his own pocket for four years. But in 1970, other funds began to come in. A board of directors had been organized to solicit funds. Some contributions came in from area churches and individuals. After finishing his book about The Way,[1] Gene decided to risk everything. He quit his job and is now devoting all his time to ministry at The Way.

Gene sees this ministry as helping youth develop a relevant faith in a Chistian community that provides them with sustenance and support. He said, "I want people to know that we are not doing social work. We're trying to say the Gospel as it really is. We are making Christians, helping them read the Bible and look for Christ in their lives, wherever he may appear."

There have been some encouraging results from the ministry of The Way. One boy who had been a glue-sniffer was able to stay off glue when he joined a family club and raise his grades in school. A boy who had been in The Way in Cambridge called as he was getting out of prison to say that he wanted to help with The Way when he got out. Another boy who had been in The Way was sent to reform school. He attended church in the town where the reform school is located, was baptized, and is now taking an active part in the church.

On a chilly morning in the fall of 1969, the first baptisms for members of The Way were held in the bay outside Quincy. Two boys, stripped to the waist, were immersed in the cold water as

---

1. *Way to Go, Baby* (Nashville: Abingdon Press, 1970).

trumpeters played "We Are One in the Spirit" and colorful banners waved in the stiff breeze. Afterward, the boys' parents and friends of The Way gathered on the rocks along the shore to celebrate communion with the newly baptized members of the youth church.

A banner on a nearby tree said, "Come on, Spirit, light my fire." The look on the boys' faces said a "fire" had been kindled within them. They had found a community of acceptance and a faith to hold on to. They had found "The Way."

In Brief

BACKGROUND

• Street youth in Cambridge needed to be related to a group in which they could develop a relevant faith, feel acceptance and love, and recognize their own worth.

• They also needed a place for recreation and "being together."

OBJECTIVE

• To minister to and with street youth, helping them develop a relevant faith and become persons able to love.

STRATEGY

• As a Harvard Divinity School student, Gene Langevin was assigned to work with a church in an area where street youth hung out.

• He developed a "drop-in" and recreation program that drew over six hundred youth.

• When the church threw the program out, a small group of youth stayed with Gene and organized The Way.

• Gene rented a storefront for The Way. Other youth were drawn to it.

• Gene took a full-time job as a probation officer in Quincy and moved The Way to a storefront in Quincy.

- Seminary students were assigned to help with the Quincy program.
- As the program drew financial support from individuals and churches, Gene was able to devote all his time to the ministry of The Way.
- The program in Quincy consists of contemporary worship, family clubs, and boys clubs.

Problems

- Conflict developed with the church housing the initial program, over the use of the building and the type of youth involved in the program.
- Financial support was very minimal for the first five years of the program. Gene paid most of the expenses from his own pocket for five years.

Results

- Many of the needs of street youth have been met, including the need for a community of acceptance where they can experience personal growth and develop a relevant faith.
- Youth have experienced "being the church" through participating in meaningful theological study, developing their own worship, and maintaining their own institution.

CHAPTER 11

Black Culture Center
Indianapolis, Indiana

The psychedelic sign says "Black Culture Center." But the gray frame building looks like a church. Inside, you find that it's both. It's the Hillside Christian Church (Disciples of Christ) in a low-income Black neighborhood of Indianapolis. One of the main thrusts of the church's ministry is the Black Culture Center.

The Center is many things. It's recreation—pool, Ping-Pong, table games—for kids who drop in. It's a modern dance class led by professional instructors. It's a voice choir, work projects, summer camp, field trips. It's a Black history class. It's a YMCA meeting during the winter and a Community Fine Arts Festival in the summer.

And more than anything else, it's drama.

The Drama Program

Mose Laderson is the minister of Hillside Christian Church. And drama is his "bag." Mose has been involved in drama all of his life. He became hooked the first time he performed, back in grade school in Mississippi.

When Mose graduated from seminary, there weren't too many churches open to Black pastors. So he took a job with a school and produced plays during his spare time. His group, called "The Laderson Players," became widely known and even received a mayor's citation.

When a job opened up at a settlement house, Mose continued producing plays. Then the United Christian Missionary Society invited him to become pastor of the Hillside Christian Church.

There were only six members in the Hillside Christian Church when Mose arrived—and $6 in the treasury. His salary was paid by the United Christian Missionary Society.

Mose started getting people together to put on plays. Many were youth, but adults also came. They worked together, spanning the generation gap through their common interest. People in the community began attending the plays, paying up to $2.50 for a performance (but Mose gave many season tickets away to persons who couldn't pay). The money went into the church treasury and it now boasts a balance of $4,000. Eighty or ninety people now attend the church service on Sunday morning. When plays are presented, the sanctuary is packed.

The players have become known in the area. They have performed for other churches in Indianapolis and surrounding cities. In 1971 they performed for the Disciples of Christ Convention.

Other churches have joined with them to present plays, and several interracial dramas have been produced in this way.

The plays are of a professional caliber. Among their productions have been "No Greater Love" by William Fisher, "Mooney's Kid Don't Cry" by Tennessee Williams, and "The Amen Corner" by James Baldwin. The Baldwin play was done with an interracial caste of forty.

The Summer Program

During the summer, activity at the Black Culture Center picks up. The community around the church has many needs and very few servicing agencies, so the Center fills the gap.

During the summer of 1970, Clarence Jordan, a student from

Tougaloo College, was hired by the United Christian Missionary Society to work with Mose in a community program. In place of the traditional Vacation Bible School, the Center held a Black Emphasis Week, which included a class in Black history, a class in the basic principles of Christianity, movies, and recreation.

The Center sponsored field trips for youth. One of these was to a recreational center in Cleveland. Before this trip, most of the youth had never been out of their neighborhood.

Other youth were recruited for an integrated camp at Indian Lake. And some attended a day camp sponsored by the Model Cities Program.

One of the highlights of the summer was a community fine arts festival. There were art exhibits, including a black wall of dignity. There was a community barbecue. There was dancing in the street to the tune of six bands as well as a slingshot contest and a bike rodeo. In the evening, the drama group at Hillside presented two one-act plays.

Clarence Jordan said about the summer: "I think this project provided one of the most formidable experiences of my life. Each day brought about a new job and a newer approach to that job. There were times when I was struck with the many problems that confront us. But there were other times that I had the satisfaction of feeling I was doing my share in trying to eliminate some of these problems."

The On-Going Ministry

During the school year, the Black Culture Center is a clubhouse for the YMCA. Professional staff use the facilities for their programs. And it's open for unsupervised recreation to kids who drop in.

There is also a voice choir, which Mose directs. And from time to time groups work on improvisational drama.

One time the improvisational group dramatized the story of Cinderella. It was an integrated group. "You'd be surprised what an integrated group will do with Cinderella," Mose said. "You could see the hostility. The kids decided who would do the parts—who would be the stepmother and the stepsisters."

A modern dance class meets at the Center, with professional instruction provided through a grant from the Disciples' Reconciliation Fund.

The Center has also sponsored interracial work projects. One group painted fourteen houses in the area, working with the residents who lived in the houses. And a group from the suburbs joined a Center group for a major street cleanup, which included planting grass the entire length of one street.

A Free Agent

Much of the program at the Center has been possible because Mose is not dependent on the church for his support. Initially, his salary was paid by the United Christian Missionary Society. At the present time he is employed as full-time director of the Northeast Citizen Action Project, a part of the Indianapolis Poverty Program.

Mose feels that this financial independence allows him the freedom to be creative in his ministry. Many of the people in the community feel that a church should not be involved in modern dance, music, and drama. "They think the church is a place to meet on Sundays and that is all," he said. "You meet the Lord there and you go on home and forget it."

But financial independence has allowed him to shape a ministry that meets real needs. At the same time, it has enabled him to build up a worshiping and serving congregation that is engaged in relevant ministry.

However, the financial independence also has its negative aspects. A full-time job limits the time Mose can spend in his church's ministry. He would like to see the Center provide supervised recreation for the drop-ins. He would like to produce more plays. He would like a more extensive summer program. But there is just so much time available.

A Kind of Soul Food

The Black Culture Center is not just a youth ministry—it's a total ministry to a total community. It's a rare example of youth and adults integrated into a program that meets everyone's needs.

The needs, as Mose Laderson sees them, are for "soul food." People in the community around Hillside are poor, but money is not the only thing they need, Mose says. They need a sense of pride, a sense of "being somebody."

They get this sense of "being somebody" through experiences in the arts. "The arts do something to you." Mose said. "They put you on the same plane as everyone else. It's interesting to know that after slavery, they didn't have Black actors. The arts make everybody equal and they didn't want that."

Most of the youth at Hillside have very little chance to develop leadership skills. At school, the only Blacks who become leaders are the few who become known in sports. But participating in drama, modern dance, and other arts helps kids to develop confidence in themselves and to take leadership they would normally shy away from.

"We have people who can't read and write very much," Mose said. "But they can memorize. After a while, they even learn to read." (Interestingly, Mose would rather work with an actor who is not a good reader, because the good reader uses less expression in reading his lines than the actor who is not used to this artificial way of speaking.)

"We also have kids who come in who are afraid to talk," Mose added. "You give them a little spotlight and it does something for their whole personality. They become more aggressive after a successful play. All people really need is a chance to express themselves."

Black Culture Center

Experiences in the arts at the Black Culture Center provide the soul food that makes people feel worthwhile. And that's a real ministry.

In Brief

BACKGROUND
- The Hillside Christian Church was dying. It had only six members, virtually no money in the treasury, and virtually no ministry to the many needs of its community.
- People in the poverty area surrounding the church had many needs, particularly the need to feel worthwhile.

OBJECTIVE
- To provide residents of the community (both youth and adults) with a sense of worth.

STRATEGY
- Mose Laderson became pastor of the Hillside Christian Church, with his salary paid by the United Christian Missionary Society.
- Because of his interest in drama, Mose developed a drama program that met the objective of the ministry.
- The drama program expanded into a Black Culture Center.
- Support for a summer assistant and an expanded summer program was provided by the United Christian Missionary Society.
- Mose now has a full-time job with the Poverty Program in Indianapolis and carries on his ministry at the church part-time.

PROGRAM
- The program includes recreation, modern dance, voice choir, work projects, a YMCA, summer camp, field trips, a Com-

munity Fine Arts Festival, a Black history class, and an extensive drama program.

PROBLEMS

• Some church members left because they did not agree with the kinds of activities provided by the center. However, many more joined the church.

• Financial independence has made possible a relevant program but it has also limited the scope of the program because Mose must hold a full-time job unrelated to the arts program.

RESULTS

• Many youth and adults have developed self-confidence and a greater sense of self-worth through participation in the arts.

• Some youth have had a place to drop in for recreation.

• Some youth have learned more about Black history and the Christian faith.

• Youth and adults have worked together, with greater understanding of each other and greater appreciation for each other.

• The community has been drawn together through work projects and festivals.

CHAPTER 12

Beechview Community Youth Program
Pittsburgh, Pennsylvania

Pittsburgh is a city of neighborhoods. One of these, Beechview, is made up of 20,000 people crowded together on the "second hill south of downtown."

Beechview was first settled around the time of the First World War. Another surge of growth came in the 1950s, when almost all the available land was put to use. Many of the residents are first- or second-generation immigrants from southern and eastern Europe. And many moved to Beechview from redevelopment areas of the city.

Because Beechview is geographically isolated from much of the rest of the city, it has maintained its strong ethnic cohesiveness and community identity. Youth, however, have rebelled against ethnic restraints and hard-hat politics. Their rebellion has been acted out in drug use, unrest at the high school, trouble with the police, and vandalism.

There is only one public piece of land in Beechview, a small triangular plot of ground on which a war memorial stands, across from the Beechview Christian Church (Disciples of Christ). A somewhat loosely organized gang of youth claimed this spot. They called themselves the Monumentals.

Sometimes the Monumentals moved over to the steps of the Christian Church. At times they broke into the church or the garage of the parsonage next door.

This vandalism was one of the first things Art Keys was confronted with when he came to Beechview as the new pastor of the Christian Church.

A Commitment to Change

Art Keys came to Beechview after one year at Yale Divinity School. He said, "It was 1968 . . . and I felt I had to get out and do something." (The year 1968 saw the assassinations of Martin Luther King, Jr., and Robert Kennedy, and the McCarthy campaign, in which Art was active.) He was given an interim assignment as pastor of the Beechview church, which was in the throes of deciding about its future as a congregation.

Art became concerned about the youth on the steps of the church and at the monument across the street. Gradually he won the confidence of the leaders of the Monumentals and, in January 1969, invited them to use the church basement for recreation.

The program caught on. Adults began to volunteer to help out in what became a drop-in center. Recreation equipment (pool tables, Ping-Pong tables, television, reading material, table games) was secured, partially from a Beechview Recreation Association that had been organized but never developed any programs.

By May, Art said, "the program had outrun me." Kids were at the church every time it was open. They were clamoring for it to be available seven days a week.

The Methodist and Presbyterian churches of Beechview were, at this time, negotiating with the Christian Church to create a summer program that would include combined worship services. They agreed also to sponsor the youth center.

Then, on July 1, the youth center developed a separate board of directors. Members were appointed from the three churches: the pastor, one adult volunteer from each church, and six youth

Beechview Community Youth Program

who were involved in the program. The Catholic churches and Lutheran churches also became involved, and for a while, the Lutherans had a section of the program at their own church.

The board of directors determined to develop a program that would provide a place for youth to go (they were constantly hassled by the police on the streets), that would provide an alternative to the drug culture, and that would attempt to bridge the age and culture gap in Beechview.

There were three aspects of the program: unstructured recreation (pool, Ping-Pong), structured recreation (dances, light shows), and education (police-community relations seminars, speeches by political candidates).

Adult volunteers were always at the center. But the Monumentals took care of disicipline. It was their place, and they maintained its order.

In August, Harold Cranston, a VISTA volunteer, was assigned to the program.

There were some problems with the program right from the beginning. Adults in the neighboring homes objected to a gathering of youth at the church. Art handled this by inviting some of them to become involved in the program themselves. Some did come to hear the mayoral candidates speak, after Art invited them in house-to-house calls.

There were problems in keeping the place clean, kids staying at the church after the program closed, and some bad press in the community.

But there were some encouraging results. Some boys scrubbed the basement room where they were meeting, cut the grass outside, and washed the sidewalks, They also held a dance and contributed the proceeds to the church.

The police-community relations seminars brought results. The crime count among juveniles in the area went down. And there was real understanding between some of the police officials and youth in the area.

Crisis and Closing

In September, the Christian Church decided to dissolve their corporation and sell their building. The majority voted to turn it over to the Christian Church (Disciples of Christ) in Pennsylvania, with the understanding that the youth center would perhaps still be maintained.

But then some crises developed. Three youth who had been involved with the center were picked up on narcotics charges and police confiscated six duffel bags of marijuana in their possession. A few weeks later, another group of teen-agers who were not related to the center but were from the community were picked up as they attempted to cure a pillowcase full of marijuana in a laundromat.

Because there was suspicion that drugs were being pushed at the center, police investigated. But of course they found nothing.

At the same time, police officials who had supported and been sympathetic to the center program and with whom the kids had developed real rapport were transferred to another section of the city and the new officials proved unsympathetic.

Community support for the program began to wane. In fact, many people became very hostile toward it. Neighbors who had resented the kids near their property called up the police with numerous complaints about what was going on at the center. A businessman in the neighborhood began an active campaign to get the center closed.

Art was asked to appear at a community council meeting. (Mrs. Hines, one of his most loyal supporters, was president of the group and wanted to give him the opportunity to explain the facts about the center.) Art gave his talk, but feelings were running strong in the audience. He felt there was a complete breakdown of communication, even though many people were backing him.

Beechview Community Youth Program

In early October, the church was officially closed, and Art closed the youth program to wait for the controversy to die down. A group organized by the businessman filed a petition to prevent the church from turning over its property to the Disciples of Christ organization, fearing it would be used again for a youth center.

A second vote on the disposition of the church property was taken on October 12. The count was essentially the same: The majority wanted to turn the property over to the state organization.

On October 14, the day before Moratorium Day, Art held a service for youth at the church, at their request. It was not a liturgical service, but more of a "talk-in." The service had barely begun when the phones began ringing. "It was unbelievable," Art said. "People were calling from the other end of town to find out what youth were doing in the church." Sensing that there might be trouble, Art concluded the service and sent the kids home.

Outside, a confrontation developed between the kids and the businessman. The police were called and the kids were lined up against a wall. Some got away, but five were arrested and taken to the police station.

Art followed and asked the arresting officer what the charges were. By demanding a charge, Art was forcing the police to either press charges or release the kids. The kids were released and Art visited their parents to explain what had happened.

A few days later, as Art told it, "I was standing on the corner across from the church talking with some kids who were working for political candidates in the coming election. The police came by and told us to get moving. Art continued talking to a few kids, and the police arrested him for loitering and disorderly conduct.

Art still doesn't believe what happened next. He was taken to night court, refused a lawyer, tried in forty-five minutes and fined $50 plus court costs or thirty days in the county workhouse.

He says, "I stood behind bars and could see a pay phone on the wall outside my cell, but I didn't have any money with me." Finally, he begged a dime from the turnkey and called Harold Cranston, the VISTA volunteer who had been assisting at the center. He came down in the morning and posted bail. Art's case was picked up by the American Civil Liberties Union and was eventually thrown out of court.

Meanwhile, the church went to court over the disposition of their property. The judge awarded it to the Christian Church (Disciples of Christ) in Pennsylvania. Art eased himself out of the picture and eventually went back to Yale.

Reopening

The youth center was dormant for a period of several months. Harold Cranston of VISTA was employed during the winter by the Welfare Rights Organization, and he kept in contact with the kids who had been involved. Then, in April, he quietly opened up the center once more.

Things went more smoothly this time. Community opposition had died down. Two other community organizations were negotiating to use the upper floors of the church building: the Community Mental Health Program and an Opportunity Center for physically and mentally retarded people. So the building was becoming, in a very real sense, a community building.

Harold remained with the program until August, when his term with VISTA expired. He returned to Stanford, where he has been instrumental in getting grants from foundations to support the Beechview program.

The new director is a former resident of the community, Francis Harris, who is attending college on the G.I. Bill and is able to work for a minimum salary.

The Family

Youth at the Beechview Community Youth Center now call themselves the Family. There is a sign on the wall that says what they've been through: Can this place be possible?

An executive of the district office of the Christian Church in Pittsburgh, Dwight French, has said, "You couldn't kill this program now if you wanted to."

The kids—and adults—have invested a lot in the center. They've weathered community controversy and hassles with the police. It's their thing and they're going to keep it alive.

In Brief

BACKGROUND

• Beechview had a rebellious youth population that acted out its problems with drugs, vandalism, and disorderly conduct at school.

• There were no youth recreation facilities in the community.

• There was an almost complete breakdown in communication between youth and adults in the community, as well as between police and youth.

OBJECTIVE

• To provide a place where youth could gather and where reconciliation might occur between generations and between youth and the police.

STRATEGY

• Art Keys opened up the basement of the Beechview Christian Church to an informal gang called the Monumentals.

- A youth center emerged.
- The program became ecumenical and a board of directors, representing the churches and youth from the program was appointed.
- When the church disbanded, some people in the community protested turning the property over to the Christian Church (Disciples of Christ) in Pennsylvania, for fear they might continue the youth program.
- The church was turned over to the Disciples of Christ state organization in a court case and, several months later, the youth center was opened again.
- The new director was hired from within the community.

PROGRAM
- Unstructured recreation was provided for drop-ins.
- Structured recreation was sometimes planned.
- Some educational programs were held.

PROBLEMS
- Alienation between generations and between the police and youth was brought out into the open and focused on the youth center.
- There were organized attempts to shut down the center.

RESULTS
- Some youth and adults were reconciled.
- Some youth and police were reconciled.
- Youth were provided with a gathering place that they could take responsibility for.
- The church faced up to problems of alienation between youth and adults.
- The church broadened its concept of ministry.

CHAPTER 13

Two Rural Ministries
Timber Lake, South Dakota
North Livermore, Maine

The urbanization of America has focused the public eye on the problems and the blessings of the cities. Through it all, however, people have continued to live on the farms and in the small towns of the nation. In many ways, their needs and even their interests are unknown to the general public. In many minds, the word rural has become synonymous with lack of opportunity, struggle, and a deteriorating social structure.

The problems in the rural areas are almost all related to a declining population base. Improved agricultural methods coupled with the encroachment of corporation farming have gradually dwindled away the family farm. Fewer people raise more produce and the economy of the open spaces and the small towns that serve them suffers.

The people who do remain in these places are the victims of the nation's increased efficiency. They are no longer able to maintain the social institutions they once had and the services rendered by the dwindling communities are curtailed. It is easy for the local people to speed over to the larger population center where the prices are cheaper.

Youth reared in this environment are particularly vulnerable. Opportunity for them lies in the cities, so they are one of rural America's chief exports.

For our study, we chose two rural communities that included one element common to most rural communities: isolation. This isolation does not succeed in shutting out the cultural pressures of American life. Mass media does penetrate the mountains and the prairies. The interaction of our industrial society with the rural populations sometimes produces outward results somewhat different from those that same interaction produces in the more populated areas. But the needs expressed by these outward results seem to be no different from those expressed by people in the cities.

The Settings

Because of the differences between these models and those found in the other chapters of the book, a brief description of the two communities follows.

TIMBER LAKE, SOUTH DAKOTA

Located in the north central area of South Dakota, Timber Lake is in the midst of the Cheyenne Indian Reservation. The town consists of one short business street and is surrounded by the vast openness of the prairies.

People who live here are at home with distance. They must travel great lengths to transact much of their business, go to school, and often even to see friends. The distances are traveled quickly because of the lack of traffic congestion, but they still contribute to the feeling of isolation for the whole area.

Cattle ranching is the main business here. Since it is dry country, the residents have discovered that it makes economic sense to provide as much grazing area for their cattle as possible. Consequently ranches have been growing larger and fewer.

Since distance is of such importance to life, "wheels" are even more sought after and used by youth than in more urban areas. The kids learn to drive at an early age and South Dakota has licensing laws that enable fourteen-year-olds to get special school driving permits. There is very little anxiety on the part of the older generation toward this possession of automobiles at an early age. It is a way of life.

Social life in places like Timber Lake has its limitations, and small groupings and gatherings take on more importance than they do in more populated areas. Youth who are involved on the family ranches and are a part of the family economic unit really face less trouble in this area of life. But sometimes those who live in the small towns find their hands too filled with time, resulting in much boredom.

Most of the youth who live here now will be gone in a few years. They look beyond Timber Lake for their future. Only a small proportion of them will return to make their homes here.

LIVERMORE FALLS, MAINE

The scene is different in Livermore Falls. The miles are not as long but the feeling of isolation can become as strong as in Timber Lake. North Livermore is set in the midst of trees. You cannot see miles in every direction and the land seems to echo the fact that at one time it fought men for every inch they took from it. North Livermore does not, in any real sense, depend on the land for its existence now. People who live in this place do their work in other towns.

Most of them live here because they choose to do so. The scenery is beautiful, the population is not very dense, there are lakes and recreation areas close by.

Nor is North Livermore completely devoid of opportunity. The neighboring towns offer opportunities for work in the mills and business firms. Yet most of the kids growing up in North Livermore will not live out their lives here. They will move out while very young and will never return to live here.

This area does offer more of an opportunity for social contacts than does Timber Lake. But to grow up in North Livermore is to face the possibility of not becoming a significant part of anything that is happening in the world. It is very possible for life here to become a beehive of meaningless activities unrelated to the real needs of people.

Two People

In both Timber Lake and North Livermore, youth ministry centers around an individual. In both places, the activities engaged in are neither controversial nor separated from the church. In both places the opportunity for talk and discussion plays a large role in the ministry. Finally, in both places a close and challenging group life has emerged that has made the ministry significant to a number of the youth involved.

JEANNIE SHERMAN

For twenty-five years, the Reverend Jeannie Sherman has been the pastor of the Timber Lake church. She came to this isolated western community from Massachusetts and her voice still contains a hint of her origins. To understand Jeannie and her ministry it is only necessary to spend an afternoon in her home. One suspects that any afternoon would suffice, as the pattern is most likely repeated daily.

People pass through. They come to prepare reports, to ask about a meeting, to suggest an approach, to seek some advice, to sit in on a class. One suspects, however, that they come because there is warmth in the home. Here is a place to talk. Here is someone who is interested in who they are.

Among them are visitors of all ages. They all stay, mingling to talk together. Each person knows the other and all know the total of what is happening in the community. In one sense that room is Timber Lake. The elements are quietly shut out and the warmth penetrates. But that room is also a window to the world beyond the prairie.

Jeannie has assumed that the kids who come through this room year after year are going to live in a place and at a pace they cannot imagine. She has recognized that the whole world is not exactly what Timber Lake is. She knows the possibility of her kids getting lost and confused in it.

The afternoons and evenings in her home, the hours of listening and talking, and the trips and public services the kids plan with Jeannie are all steps in their weaning from isolation.

None of the activities in this rural parish could be called radical by anyone. The kids have an ecumenical youth group. They plan services which they call contemporary. They talk a lot. They wonder about the things they know are happening in the world. They express their own feelings about those events. And maybe because they have someone who listens to what they think, and who leads them out of their immediate surroundings, they are a little more open to life than the average teen-ager.

And maybe they are a little more prepared for whatever happens to them later. Somehow a lot of kids whose educational background is not as extensive as that received in urban systems do not find the adjustment to that other world as difficult as might be expected.

BILLIE JEAN GAMMON

Nothing about Billie Jean is radical, though some people think differently. She is a housewife whose family has grown. She happens to live in North Livermore. The ministry she has encouraged there is one that reaches out from the community but also reaches deeply into the community.

The vehicle for her ministry is the local Baptist youth fellowship of which she has become the adviser. But the ministry is to and with any persons of any age living within that community and beyond. The youth fellowship has become an outreach group. It is a group that has been built in trust.

Activities consist of things like planned excursions to the state reformatory and to the Chinese Baptist church in Boston. Each excursion has behind it more than the idea of a trip away from the old home town or satisfying the curiosity of some kids from an isolated place in Maine. With each excursion the group adds to itself an increased understanding of the world beyond it.

In the months preceding an excursion, the fellowship group spends many hours acquainting itself with the problems and conditions surrounding the place and the people they are about to visit. They correspond with the people in that place, asking the questions that rise from their own study. By the time they are ready to leave, their minds are curious and they are anxiously waiting to meet the people they have only heard of and face problems they could never have understood in any other way.

Correspondence continues after the visit is over. The youth ask themselves what they can do to help potential reformatory candidates. They wonder about their future relationship to the inner city. An important result of their visiting and their wondering is that this group has become the kind of group the very people who need them can trust.

The excursions within the community are more than just the parties and the strangely named excursions Billie Jean helps them plan and name. The ones that any member of the group will tell you really matter are those that have been planned to help the lives of some people in and around North Livermore.

The conservative town, for instance, had difficulty accepting a divorcé who was living out his own lonely existence there. The kids moved in. They became his life and he became a part of theirs.

A German war bride settled in North Livermore. She is confronted by proselytizing religious groups eager to change her to what they are. But she does not want that kind of change. She is a person in a new land with all the loneliness that implies. The befriending she needs comes not from a neighboring lady over coffee but from this group of kids who make her one of them. No questions asked. No demands made.

Such stories really abound in North Livermore. And these

excursions, discussed and evaluated over Cokes and doughnuts in as many different settings as there are places where kids gather, become the program.

Not that there is no fun in the group. It has become a social group for some kids in what could otherwise be a lonely place. But equally, it has equipped them with an understanding of the importance of trust and understanding. They have seen the difference those values have brought about in the lives of people whom they have come to know.

Billie Jean has a feel for the kids and for the people of the community. She has developed the ability to notice the little things that are important to people.

One of the stories told is that often when the boys go hunting for rabbits or other small game, they bring the results of the hunt to Billie before they show it to anyone else. It's an easy thing to understand. Billie does not slight them or push off their accomplishments. She recognizes the importance of their thing, no matter how small it may seem to the rushing world surrounding them.

Needs of a community do not spring from the bushes and stand full blown in the sunlight. Billie Jean and the group, which now consists of both adult and youth members, scour their community for its needs. At the time of this writing, they were concentrating on the personal needs of selected individuals.

Their conception of the social needs of groups has been opened by their excursions to the cities and reformatories. And they can somewhat grasp the need for massive changes to bring about some semblance of humanity in the world.

Conclusion

Perhaps the youth and adults in these two rural ministries reflect a unique breed of people for this day. Living in the 1970s and keenly aware of all of its problems because of the media, they also live in places where a former way of life still clings on.

They are faced with the problems of drug abuse but their chief concern is still with the problems of alcohol abuse. They are aware of the problems of crowding but their nearest neighbor may be twenty miles away. They have seen and heard of the great inequities of poverty and affluence, but they can ferret out only a very few of its victims in their own communities. They read about crowded schools, but their own schools are looking for students.

Most of all, they are aware that though they are growing up in such a community, the majority of their lives will be lived somewhere else. This somewhere else is different from that of an urban youth knowing he will live in a different city or in another section of the country. The somewhere else where these youth will live will be completely different in its basic nature from where they are now.

They are well aware that people living in rural America are a minority. They pick up from their parents the view that their lives are regulated from somewhere else, that the glamour lies somewhere else, and the opportunity lies somewhere else.

To minister with kids like this certainly must involve what both of these groups have attempted: acquainting them with that "somewhere else" where they will live.

In Brief

BACKGROUND
- Both rural areas are isolated by natural barriers.
- Both rural areas are well aware of the total unrest in our nation because of their own exposure to mass media.
- There is a need in both areas for a support group.
- There is a need in both areas for personalization of the world beyond.
- It is assumed in both places that the majority of the young people will eventually live somewhere else.

Two Rural Ministries

OBJECTIVE:

• To build a community of trust that will personalize the world beyond and reach out to the world close at hand.

STRATEGY

• Two adults built a trustful relationship with some youth over a period of years.

• The adults and the youth leadership searched the community to discover persons who needed the group's trust.

• The youth and adult leadership searched in the world beyond for opportunities to broaden their horizons.

• The thrust of the group was to reach out with trust and care to whoever needed and accepted it.

PROGRAM

• The searching of the community and the world beyond became the content around which discussion and learning took place.

• Opportunities were created for the youth to have time to carry out these discussions in convenient settings (the local school before or after class, a local restaurant, a home).

• The social life was planned around the needs of the persons in the trust community (a visit to someone who needed company, a picnic when someone needed the diversion).

• Public expression of the group's direction became the focal point for further discussion and planning in appropriate settings.

• The group planned excursions into the world beyond by intensely studying the place to which they were going and discussing it, preparing themselves for the experience.

• The trips were planned so that every effort was made to personalize the place and the people.

• Further community activities were encouraged by letters from the people they had seen, by projects, and by the places they had seen.

Problems
- People of the community had some difficulty understanding the relationships that the group encouraged. Many of the people to whom the group attempted to minister were unacceptable to the community itself.
- The group had most success in ministry with individuals who were the victims of social injustice. It had much difficulty in facing the problems that caused the injustice in the first place.

Results
- The results are difficult to pin down. This is especially true of the objective of preparing the youth to live in another place. Once they move, they are scattered. The only tangible evidence of the help they have received is the letters both of these women receive from the people who have left. There are many such letters thanking them for what they have given.
- In Timber Lake, there has developed an ecumenical and broad searching on the part of the youth who live in an area where such searching would be more frowned upon than accepted.
- In North Livermore, there has developed a definite trust group. It has reached out to people of all ages and has become for some the only humanizing force in their lives.

CHAPTER 14

Summer Lawn-in Melrose, Massachusetts

The First Baptist Church of Melrose, Massachusetts, is located on the edge of the business district. City hall and a fire station are across the street. Diagonally across the intersection at the edge of the church's property are a row of stores.

For years, the summer pastime of many Melrose youth was to walk up and down in front of these stores, gather on the corner, and sit on the lawn of the First Baptist Church.

In the summer of 1968, with concern rising about hippie confrontations on the nearby Boston Common and with mounting complaints from older citizens that they "no longer felt safe walking to the stores because the kids might knock them down," the city passed an ordinance banning teen-agers from congregating on Main Street, including the church lawn.

Believing that human need was the beginning of ministry, the churches of Melrose decided it was time to act. Youth were on the streets because they wanted, and needed, to be with each other. The ban on Main Street would not eliminate this need.

In the early spring of 1969, Karen Primm, a returned Peace Corp volunteer, was hired by the ministerial association to develop a summer youth program for the community. Together with leaders from the churches, she went to work on the challenge and came up with a "lawn-in." The community's youth would simply be invited to spend their evenings on the lawn of the First Baptist Church, with a minimum of program.

Organizing for Ministry

Planning began with a meeting of representatives from the city's Protestant and Catholic churches. Nine churches sent a staff person, a lay adult, and a youth to the first meeting.

Karen said, "In the beginning there was no general agreement as to what the program should be. In my own mind, it was going to be a daytime program. But it turned out to be a night program. I think we would have been way off base if it had been all adults on the committee, or all church staff. By the time we were a working committee the kids were the leaders. They were really in touch with what was happening."

The idea of opening the lawn to youth of the community was a natural for meeting the objectives of the group's ministry. Youth were already using the lawn as a meeting place. It would provide an outdoor program, which was logical during the hot summer. It was an informal spot, permitting a low-key program. It was large enough to hold the potential group of youth that might be involved.

But selling the idea to the churches and the community was not quite as natural. Questions were raised about damage to the lawn. The stained-glass window in the front of the church might be broken. There might be fights, especially if kids from other towns found out about the program and came over.

Some people were concerned about "how it would look to have kids like that all over the lawn." Some worried about drugs being pushed. Businessmen worried about business dropping off because people would be afraid to come downtown.

The committee took great pains to answer all the questions and to get as much support as possible for the project. They won approval from the Deacons and Trustees of the First Baptist

Church to use the property. They held open meetings with members of the community to answer questions. They talked to aldermen, to the mayor, and to the police. They published a newsletter explaining the program and reporting on its progress. They petitioned for, and received, an evening ban on parking in front of the church to facilitate the movement of traffic.

Their stock answer to the question of damage to property was: "If there's any trouble, we'll stop the program immediately."

Doug Cruger, associate minister of First Baptist, said, "Frankly we didn't know if there would be property damage or not. Anything could happen. But we were prepared to take the risk. And we meant what we said about stopping the program." As things worked out, no trouble developed, and the program continued through Labor Day.

Financing the program was another task of the committee. They secured contributions of $500 each from five of the larger churches. Other churches donated money for the program. The major expense was Karen's salary. Program and promotion expense was minimal.

The Program

The committee planned a very unstructured program for the 150 to 300 youth who came to the lawn each evening. Movies were shown Monday and Thursday nights. On Wednesdays some faculty members from the Massachusetts College of Pharmacy led a seminar on drugs. Friday evenings there was a rock concert. On Sunday, Tuesday, and Saturday, a record player and large television were available. Informal dramas were sometimes held.

Kids often provided their own entertainment. The vast majority just sat around and talked. (One adult commented:

"I've never seen such massive inactivity!") Some played Frisbee, listened to records, played catch with a ball or balloon, or played their guitars.

Each of the sponsoring churches took responsibility for providing chaperons. Their job was to be available in case the kids needed them. Some joined in discussions with the youth. Others simply watched, and learned about youth culture.

The Results

The trouble the townspeople had feared did not develop. The program ran from June 13 through Labor Day and there were only a few incidents.

Some teen-agers brought beer or were intoxicated when they arrived. They were escorted off the grounds. One night a gang from another town arrived and challenged some kids on the lawn to a fight. The police were called and the gang moved on. Occasionally a fight would break out on the lawn but other kids persuaded them to fight somewhere else; they were very protective of "their" lawn.

At first the main trouble came from the police, who had been apprehensive of the project from the beginning. They moved up and down the sidewalk in front of the church, telling the youth to keep their feet on the lawn and off the sidewalk. After four or five nights, kids on the lawn picked up the chant "feet off the sidewalk" whenever they saw a cop approaching. Leaders decided to talk with the police chief and this situation was soon corrected. In fact, the police became strong allies of the program before the summer was over.

Another source of trouble was a new local newspaper that was competing for readership. On the front page they printed complaints about the program from the police blotter. Leaders of the lawn ministry talked with the editor and sent positive news stories and soon the paper became a major factor in developing community support for the program.

Summer Lawn-in

There were very few dramatic results of the lawn ministry, but it was a significant attempt to minister to youth who had a lot of time on their hands. The trouble that was anticipated downtown as a result of the Main Street ban did not develop. Youth had a place to go where they were accepted and were allowed to be themselves. They learned to be responsible for their behavior and for "their" property. Adults learned that youth could be responsible. The community learned that a mass gathering of youth did not have to be destructive.

Perhaps most important, youth began talking to each other and to adults. Even factions among the city's youth that had often been involved in fighting each other found themselves sitting on the same lawn together and sometimes carried on mutual conversations.

Did the youth feel it was a success? Their comments seem to indicate it.

One boy said, "This is a lot better than last year. We were getting sick of the police saying you can't stay here and you can't go there."

Another boy said, "I used to hang out behind the fire station with a few guys. But there wasn't much to do other than play catch and if there were too many of us the neighbors would complain and the cops would come. This is a hundred percent better."

A girl said, "The lawn is a good place to go without really being hassled, but I think one day at least should be spent in cleaning up the lawn and giving it a lot of water. If the lawn dies, so does the lawn ministry."

The lawn didn't die, and neither did the lawn ministry. It expanded into a year-round program. Karen was hired and the committee began searching for an inside home for the ministry during the winter. Eventually a Youth Commission was established by the aldermen, composed of both adults and youth.

And the lawn-in was held again the next summer.

In Brief

BACKGROUND
- Youth needed a place where they could be together informally. They had been prohibited from meeting on Main Street.
- The ban on Main Street was a potential threat to youth-adult relationships in the community.

OBJECTIVE
- To provide a place where community youth could meet informally.

STRATEGY
- A committee of youth, adults, and staff members from nine community churches was organized.
- A full-time staff person was hired to plan and direct the summer program.
- The churches funded the program.
- The committee planned the structure, publicized the program, solicited community support, arranged for chaperons, and evaluated the results.

PROGRAM
- The lawn of the First Baptist Church was opened to community youth every night of the week from June 13 to Labor Day.
- Youth provided their own activities, such as Frisbee, guitars, listening to records, watching television, and playing ball.
- A few mass activities were scheduled: movies, drug seminars, informal dramas, and rock concerts.

PROBLEMS
- The community was suspicious of youth gatherings.
- The church was concerned about property damage.

Summer Lawn-in

- Businessmen were concerned about business loss.
- Initially, there was a lack of police cooperation.
- There was unfavorable publicity early in the program.

RESULTS

- Youth were provided with a place where they could meet informally. From 150 to 300 youth were on the lawn each night.
- Youth talked to youth, even members of rival factions.
- Adults and youth talked with one another.
- Youth learned that the churches of the city cared what happened to them.
- The city learned that a mass gathering of youth could be disciplined and constructive.

CHAPTER 15

The Peace Pipers
Ravenna, Ohio

When four students were killed at Kent State University in the spring of 1970, Father Carl Kish counseled with their families. As a chaplain at the nearest hospital, in Ravenna, Ohio, he also counseled with the injured. And, as assistant at the Immaculate Conception Church, he helped Ravenna youth through the shock and bitterness of the week's events.

Ravenna, like most communities surrounding Kent State, became more rigidly polarized following the National Guard incident. Youth were pitted against adults, "long hairs" against "straights," peace groups against patriots.

But here and there small signs of reconciliation began to appear among the townspeople. One was the "Walk for the Poor" sponsored by the youth of the Immaculate Conception Church, which brought together over two hundred people, from eight years old to fifty, in an effort to raise money for poverty programs.

Another sign of reconciliation was the response of the community to a group of folk singers from the church who called themselves the Peace Pipers.

A Slow Beginning

Actually, the Peace Pipers had been around since 1966. They were organized when Father Joseph Tamburrini, then assistant at Immaculate Conception, gathered together a group of youth to develop a folk mass. The mass was presented on Wednesday nights, and it took a while for it to catch on.

Diane Dugan, who was in the group at that time, said, "When we started, none of us knew whether we liked this kind of music in church. At first we packed all of seven to ten people in on a Wednesday night."

When Father Kish came to the parish, he moved the mass to the Attic (a teen center in the parish school) and combined it with the confraternity of Christian Doctrine classes. Five or six families attended, along with the high school students involved in the CCD classes.

In the spring of 1969, the folk group moved back to the church and sang for one mass each Sunday. The music began to catch on. People began coming from all over the area, and soon the folk mass was packed. All five hundred seats in the church were full and as many as two hundred more worshipers crammed the aisles.

Diane said, "It seems people understand that we enjoy being in church, and they do too."

The group added a second mass, for grade school children. Folk music in the church had finally been accepted—and appreciated.

Going Public

In the fall of 1970, the group decided to "go public," and they made a long-playing record.

Father Kish said, "I thought our group was as good as a lot of the groups you hear singing religious folk music, and I wanted others to hear us."

Others did hear the group. The record caught on with people all over the community and as far away as Cleveland and Canton, Ohio.

Two Cleveland television stations approached the group to

It's Happening with Youth

do programs. A church in Canton approached them to do an ecumenical service, as well as a service for a Catholic church.

Father Kish is an enthusiastic public relations man for the group. He said, "I'm going to write to Ed Sullivan. I figure we might as well go all the way; what have we got to lose?"

But getting known is not the primary purpose of the group. Youth see it as a way of expressing their faith and as a way of helping others find relevance in the church.

A very personal faith is expressed in some of the original songs written by members of the group and performed on their record.

Terry Palmer, one of the original members of the group, wrote many of the songs. One, "When I See," talks about God's love: "When I feel lost and really all alone, like I've been trapped and never will get home, He takes my hand and shows me what a comfort it can be . . ."

Among the other songs on the record are: "They'll Know We Are Christians by Our Love," "Shout from the Highest Mountain," and "Battle Hymn of the Republic."

Diane, who has remained with the group but has also enjoyed other musical success—such as being a member of Bob Hope's chorus one summer—said, "We chose the songs people most enjoyed singing."

The record was produced through a local company. Father Kish says if he had it to do over again, he would seek more advice first about the mechanics of getting a record produced. He feels they spent more money than was really necessary and perhaps would have gotten better quality with a studio production.

Their record was produced from a tape that was recorded in the basement of the church. The tape was then sent to a company who produced 5,000 plastic discs at a cost of $1,500. Another $200 was spent on record covers. The records were sold for $1.50 each, so over 1,000 had to be sold to break even.

Taping the record took about two and a half hours, and another two and half hours were spent editing the tapes. There were many rehearsals to prepare for the tape. A lot of rehearsing also goes into the group's personal appearances. But the rules about rehearsals, as well as the rehearsals themselves, are very relaxed.

Anyone who wants to can join the group for singing at the mass. But if they want to appear in a program, they must rehearse.

There is no designated director of the group; no adult is in charge (Father Kish can't even read music!) Terry said, "We just decide beforehand how we want to do it, then we do it." (However, for television appearances, Terry and Diane have acted as directors.)

It is probably this looseness that creates a spirit in the group that is contagious. The group radiates real joy. Life is great, they know what they believe, and they celebrate it in song.

More Meaning in the Mass

Youth in the church are usually on the receiving end of ministry. They are entertained, taught, and served. But the Peace Pipers have turned the tables around. They are ministering to adults and each other.

Adults have found meaning in the music of youth as it is communicated in the folk mass. Mike Marino said, "I even think the old people want the mass. At first they didn't—a lot of old people didn't like it. But now this is the best mass we have." (There are seven masses each Sunday morning at Immaculate Conception. Two are folk masses: one for everyone and one for grade school children.)

Some youth are finding church has more meaning when the Peace Pipers sing in the folk mass. Kathy Metzger said, "Before, it was kind of boring to go to church, to sit there and listen to the organ grinding away. Now it's more interesting and lively."

Father Kish feels the Peace Pipers are happy with what they do and this brings a note of happiness and relaxation to the whole mass. "It's just a different atmosphere," he said. "The prayers and the mass are the same. But it's the atmosphere that's different."

Changing to a folk mass has made some youth think about the whole meaning of worship. Mike Marino said, "The music does something for the mass but it still can't cancel out the separation between the altar and the people. I think the mass should be changed today. I've told Father this before. I think mass should be like a small gathering where people can just read Scripture and discuss it and maybe have music. You should just be yourself and feel free to express your ideas to the other people. It should be more of a sharing."

Diane said the folk mass has made people more aware of the meaning of the words that are said in mass. And it has brought people together. People are really celebrating. "That's as it should be," she says. "Church is supposed to be happy, not solemn."

Bringing people together in celebration is one step toward the peace the folk group put into their name. It's a big mission, but the Peace Pipers have seen some of it accomplished.

In Brief

BACKGROUND

- Youth, and some adults, found little meaning in the traditional mass.
- Like most communities, there was a lack of communication between youth and adults in Ravenna.

OBJECTIVE

- To make the Christian faith, including worship, relevant to youth.
- To break down barriers between youth and adults.

The Peace Pipers

STRATEGY

- Father Tamburrini organized a folk group that sang at a Wednesday evening mass. Attendance was poor.
- When Father Kish came to the church, he moved the mass to the church's teen center. Attendance was still poor.
- The group was moved back to the church and they sang on Sunday mornings. Attendance increased to the point where the church was packed.
- The group developed a second mass for grade school children.
- The group became known as the Peace Pipers and produced a record.
- The record brought invitations for television performances and programs in nearby towns.

PROGRAM

- The Peace Pipers lead the music in two folk masses each Sunday: one for adults and one for elementary children.
- They also have appeared several times on television, made a long-playing record, and appeared in concert.

PROBLEMS

- The music did not catch on at first when performed in a Wednesday night mass.
- There were many problems in producing the record due to lack of experience.

RESULTS

- Youth and adults were brought together in a common celebration, using contemporary music.
- Adults gained an appreciation of the music of youth culture.
- Youth had an opportunity to minister to adults and to each other.
- Youth and adults found more relevance in their faith.

CHAPTER 16

Kamp Kachess
Easton, Washington

The mountains are only a short drive from Seattle, but they embrace an entirely different kind of world. The blare of traffic, dirt of industrial waste, and pressures from street-corner gangs are gone. In the solitude of snow-laden firs and fresh ski trails, a boy has time to think and find himself.

This is one of the reasons that the Reverend and Mrs. Wilbur Skaggs chose the mountains to develop a group home for boys. They found the spot to develop nine miles outside of Easton, Washington, in the heart of the Central Cascades. And they named it Kamp Kachess.

Meeting a Need

Wilbur Skaggs first saw the need for a group home while serving as pastor of the Woodland Park Church of God in Seattle. In counseling boys in his congregation and community, he found many who were getting into trouble because of unhealthy home environments.

One day, while driving in the mountains, Wilbur spotted a For Sale sign on the property near Easton. He stopped to investigate. There was a log building that had served as a private resort and then as a roadhouse. It was not in very good repair.

Vandals had broken in, the roof leaked, and water had run down the inside walls.

But Wilbur saw the building's possibilities and began searching for funds to purchase it. Some close friends caught his vision and joined with him to make the purchase possible. A nonprofit corporation was set up and a board of directors appointed.

The Church of God Association of Western Washington saw possibilities in using the site for year-round camping. They invested part of the proceeds from the sale of an undeveloped camp property in return for first-priority use of the mountain camp. This was a major factor in enabling the Kamp Kachess program to move ahead.

Support came for the project from many sources, many of them within Wilbur's congregation. The building was repaired, a staff was hired, and the home was licensed by the State of Washington Department of Public Assistance as a group home for boys. It opened its doors in 1964.

A Permanent Residence

Up to twenty-four boys live at the Kamp. They are all in their teens and all come voluntarily to the residence.

Boys may be referred to the home by pastors, state institutions for child care, caseworkers, and so forth. But they must visit the Kamp and request to stay there. None are committed there by others.

Once at the Kamp, the boys become a permanent part of the family, accepting all the benefits and responsibilities that that involves. They are assigned maintenance tasks around the Kamp and on the nearby Circle Double-K Ranch that has recently been purchased. They care for chickens, gardens, and livestock. They help prepare meals and clean up afterward. They chop wood for the huge fireplace in the lodge. On weekends, they are paid extra for helping with groups that rent the lodge. (Guests pay about $12 for two nights and six meals at the Kamp.)

During the school year, the boys attend public school in Easton. After school and chores, there is skiing, skating, pool, Ping-Pong, and table games, or time for quiet talks by the fire with one of the permanent staff or a caseworker who drops by. An evening hour of supervised study for homework is part of each school day.

A Ministry of Many

Getting the Kamp off the ground was not easy. None of the staff had ever been involved in a project like this before. Wilbur was trying to carry it on while maintaining all of his pastoral duties at Woodland Park. Money was a big problem. But, slowly, things were worked out.

The Woodland Park church provided the salary for a resident boys' supervisor, Dave Allen, for a year and a half. They named him minister of youth, with responsibility for working with dependent boys at Kamp Kachess. When Dave left, the Kamp was able to pick up the salary for the new supervisor, Carl "Sarge" Lewis.

Purchasing the Circle Double-K Ranch ten miles east of the Kamp proved to be a good investment. Much of the food for the Kamp is produced here.

Some support comes from leasing the facilities to "any organization that will respect the Christian character of the operation." The lodge is in great demand for ski camps and winter retreats. This association of weekend campers with resident boys provides a unique "therapy" for the boys, who have been deprived of many wholesome social contacts.

In addition to money, there have been many useful gifts from volunteers. A ski shop gave the boys complete ski outfits (skis, bindings, boots, and poles) one year. A Kiwanis Club in Seattle provided the down payment on a Chevy van. During July and August of 1970, dentists in Yakima and the Dental School of the University of Washington provided complete dental care for each boy.

Many volunteers sponsor activities for the boys outside the Kamp. During the summer of 1970, the Wenatchee Church of God hosted the boys for a pot-luck dinner followed by waterskiing. A civilian engineer at the Bremerton Naval Shipyards set up a tour of the Post Support Ship *Detroit*. And a member of the Kamp Kachess Board of Directors led seven of the boys on a trail hike.

In 1969, Wilbur Skaggs resigned his pastorate in Seattle to devote full time to the Kamp and the Ranch. The ministry was finally off the ground.

As the program reached its 1970 capacity of twenty-four boys in full-time residence, staff requirements also expanded. In addition to the executive director and office staff, three resident male supervisors were employed. A full-time cook is on duty as well as a person to manage the laundry and provide relief cooking. A resident manager at the ranch provides additional or relief supervision. A social caseworker provides the necessary file data on each boy to make possible helpful planning for him and his future. Besides these nine full-time people, an additional nine-plus persons offer part-time and volunteer service to relieve the staff, giving counseling, tutoring, maintenance, and secretarial assistance.

What Home Can Be

Many teen-agers who live in intolerable home situations today are running away, taking drugs, even commiting suicide. The boys at Kamp Kachess could be among them. But they are lucky.

Because Wilbur and Evelyn Skaggs had a dream, and a church supported them in it, these boys have a chance to learn what home can be—and what they, themselves, can become.

They bring their problems with them. There are some tense times when the problems break out into the open. Some don't make it in the open setting of the Kamp and have to be returned to the more controlled environment of an institution.

But most boys find Kamp Kachess a place where they can live on a regular schedule and with consistent discipline, and, most important, with people who care.

In Brief

BACKGROUND

- In his counseling, Wilbur Skaggs saw the need for a group home for boys.

OBJECTIVE

- To provide a group home for boys.

STRATEGY

- The Skaggs looked for a site in the mountains, finding one near Easton, Washington.
- The Western Washington Church of God Association sold its campground to make basic funds for purchase available. The site was also seen as suitable for the association's camps.
- Additional funds were secured from interested individuals.
- A board of directors was appointed.
- The buildings were repaired and Kamp Kachess was licensed as a group home for boys.
- A staff was hired.
- Later, a nearby ranch was purchased to provide food for the Kamp and additional facilities.
- The Kamp was opened to outside groups for skiing, camping, and retreats, providing additional funds.

Kamp Kachess

PROGRAM

- Kamp Kachess is a group home for boys that provides family relationships and responsibilities.

PROBLEMS

- It was difficult to secure the initial funds.
- The staff faced some problems in working out its philosophy, but none were serious.

RESULTS

- Boys from unhealthy home environments have been provided with a home where they can explore their own worth.
- The church gained an understanding of the demands of real ministry with youth.
- The community gained an understanding of boys with problems, as the boys attended its schools and became a part of its activities.

CHAPTER 17

"Somebody Cares" Hot Line
Silver Spring, Maryland

The little white card will fit in your wallet. You put it there, just in case. And when that problem comes along that you just can't handle alone, you pull it out:

SOMEBODY CARES
When people get too far down, or too far up, we try to help. We'll rap with anybody about anything from eight in the evening until two in the morning.

in an emergency
CALL PASTOR DAVID   588–5440

Pastor David, or a member of his volunteer counseling staff, answers the hot line number. He listens a lot, counsels a little, maybe refers you to a place where you can get long-term help. And your problem is just a little lighter, because "somebody cares."

A Suburban Crisis Center

Why a hot line in the suburbs? David Shaheen, associate pastor of the St. Luke Lutheran Church in Silver Spring, Maryland, thinks it is needed.

"When I first came on the staff here," he said, "I could always tell when school was over because my phone would start ringing. And a lot of kids came in to see me. I figured that if there were that many kids who would look up someone to talk with, there must be thousands out there who didn't have anyone to talk with. So we started 'Somebody Cares.'"

While at a conference in Minneapolis, David saw a telephone counseling service in operation. He studied the project and then developed his own model.

Three phones were installed in the basement of a building owned by the church. (The location of the building, as well as the identity of the counselors, is kept anonymous.) A staff of "people who care" was recruited.

Youth of the church helped to publicize the program. They placed two hundred posters in their schools and in community businssses. They handed out the wallet-sized cards or placed them in lockers. During the summer they developed bumper stickers, which were placed on cars.

Since the hot line began operating in 1970, there have been an average of a hundred calls a week.

People Who Care

The volunteers who man the operation of Somebody Cares come from many backgrounds. There are doctors, psychiatrists, clinical psychologists, school teachers, probation officers, college students, and six high school students. The one thing these people have in common is that "they care."

Recruiting volunteers has not been a problem. Most of the people who are presently involved offered their services when they heard about the program. About half of the staff belong to St. Luke.

There are approximately thirty-seven persons on the volunteer staff. Each commits himself to working one three-hour period each week. The service operates from 8 P.M. to 2 A.M., so there are two shifts each night. David tries to have three people on the 8 to 11 shift and two on the 11 to 2 shift.

All potential volunteers are screened. David only accepts those who can "express their deep feelings with words." All volunteers are required to go through an orientation program that is directed by a volunteer with a master's degree in counseling.

The orientation consists of two-hour sessions held once a week for three weeks. After the formal sessions, volunteers listen in on the phones for two weeks. Then, when they feel ready, they take their first calls. As many as two-thirds of the prospective volunteers never make it to their first call. Those who do become active volunteers are continuously evaluated throughout their service on the phones.

One way volunteers are evaluated—and helped to become more effective—is through log sheets that are carefully filled out after each call. David goes over these sheets daily and checks any questionable material with the counselors on duty.

The log sheets list the name of the caller (if it is given, and it is usually only a first name), his age, where the caller goes to school (if given), the type of problem, the counselor's evaluation of the problem (including an evaluation of the caller's feelings about the problem), and finally the action the counselor recommended.

Each log sheet is assigned a number that is registered in a master log book. Then, if a person calls a second time, the counselor can get his history by checking the master log book under the date and time of his first call.

An Exceptional Number of Problems

Many people think youth in the suburbs don't have problems, especially youth in affluent suburbs like Silver Spring. But the volunteers at Somebody Cares know the opposite is true. Although some calls come from D.C. and Virginia, most of the calls are from the Silver Spring area. And there are, David said, an "exceptional number of problems."

The largest number of calls are about boy-girl relations. "We don't have any answers for these," one of the volunteers said. "Who's the expert? What we try to do is help the caller think through the problem, look at it from all sides, and make up his or her own mind."

Fifteen percent of the calls are about drugs. Some callers are on drugs and want to get off. Some are high and want to come down. Some just want information.

One caller was terrified that he would "freak out" from a combination of LSD and beer. The counselor kept his call on "hold" and checked out the facts with one of the consulting M.D.'s on another line. In a matter of minutes he could tell the caller that the mix would not lead to a psychotic breakdown. Then, as the caller relaxed, the counselor could get into a deep discussion about the problems that led to the crisis.

Many callers ask for drug information, like the caller who said, "I just took a long purple pill with a red stripe on it; what will it do to me?"

"The hardest drug problems are the kids on heroin," David said. "One girl calls and she is just a vegetable. She has a sixty-dollar-a-day habit. She steals to keep it up. When she calls, she doesn't talk. She needs someone to talk to her."

One boy on smack called and decided to cold turkey. He asked if the counselor would "hang in there and help." He called every night for a week and, David said, "the agony, pain, and nausea were real bad." But the counselors helped get him through it.

Some calls are about family problems. One counselor played referee one night while a mother and daughter battled things out on extension phones.

A large number of calls are about medical problems: pregnancies, VD, abortions. And some are from potential suicides. One boy called long distance and talked seriously about suicide. The counselor convinced him to come in person for help. The boy hitched a ride and arrived at dawn to meet the senior pastor at St. Luke.

Volunteers use a suicide probability scale to ask potential suicides key questions. The answers indicate their suicide potential and the "very probables" get a lot of attention.

Most callers very much want to talk to someone about their problems, but they are anxious, too. Some begin by saying, "I have a friend who has this problem. . . ." Others, especially drug users, are afraid their identity might somehow become known. They are assured that their confidences are as safe as in a confessional with a priest.

Referrals are sometimes made to community services or consulting personnel related to Somebody Cares. Each volunteer has an index beside his phone with entries for such things as abortion, alcoholism, drugs, employment, hospital, housing, legal aid, medical, police-fire, pregnancy, psychiatric clinics, psychiatric help, runaways, suicide, and VD. Each entry includes community agencies, special referrals, and instructions for the volunteers. New information goes up on the bulletin board.

When You Really Care

There are many limitations to a telephone crisis center, but also many benefits. It's convenient, quick, and anonymous. It's only a starting point in solving problems, but it may help people take the important first step.

David feels the church should be involved in this kind of service because "church people do a lot of talking about caring." St. Luke supports Somebody Cares with a $2,400-a-year item in the budget (which pays for phone bills and publicity). Additional funds come from speaking engagements by members of the staff and consulting services by the staff. (David helped set up a similar service at George Washington University.)

"Somebody Cares" Hot Line

Volunteers feel their unpaid status helps their message become authentic. "A caller asks if we get paid and we say no. This convinces them that we really care. Why else would we be here all night?"

A volunteer said, "One girl asked me why I did this sort of thing. I told her. She asked if this is a church-run operation and I said it is. Anyway, she pressed me as to why I did it, and I blurted out, 'I guess I do it because of Christ.' I'm not used to talking that away, and the idea kind of amazed me, but now I can tell them openly if they ask me, I do it for Christ."

The volunteers do not always know what happens to the kids who call in—whether they seek the help they have been referred to, whether they go off drugs or make up with their boyfriend. But once in a while, word gets back that the call made a difference in someone's life.

In Brief

BACKGROUND

- Many youth in the St. Luke Lutheran Church sought out Pastor David Shaheen for counseling. He sensed that many more youth in the community needed crisis counseling.
- There were resource people in the congregation and community who could provide crisis counseling on a volunteer basis.

OBJECTIVE

- To provide crisis counseling for youth in the Silver Spring area.

STRATEGY

- David Shaheen observed a crisis telephone service in operation in Minneapolis.
- He developed an adaptation of the model he had observed.

- Volunteer staff were recruited from the congregation and community.
- Staff were trained by David Shaheen and a qualified volunteer.
- Youth in the congregation helped develop and distribute publicity.
- The program is funded by the church and coordinated by David Shaheen.

PROBLEMS

- Coordination of staff is the largest problem. David feels this could be a full-time job.
- Followup on calls and improving resources is also a full-time responsibility.

RESULTS

- Youth in Silver Spring and surrounding communities have been provided with crisis counseling.
- Volunteers (including some youth volunteers) have had an opportunity to express their faith in tangible service.
- The church has become aware of the problems youth face in their community.

The Future

CHAPTER 18

Conflict with the Institutional Church

We have tried to show in the preceding chapters that relevant youth ministry can be created to respond to the needs of today's youth.

This ministry involves careful planning. It means developing new skills and becoming committed to a creative process and an emerging design. And it means approaching youth ministry from an entirely new perspective: that of sharing in the search for faith in which youth are already engaged.

The case studies have been provided as examples of the kinds of youth ministry that can be created and as illustrations of the process through which the different forms have developed. They have not been provided as models for others to duplicate. We cannot stress too much that each group needs to find its own form of ministry, and to go through the process of creating it, in order for it to be relevant.

The case studies have also been provided to illustrate the pain that sometimes is involved in creating new forms of youth ministry. These ministries have developed as a direct response to the tremendous social revolution existing in our time, and persons who participate in this revolution cannot avoid the pain that goes with it.

Some of the pain might be alleviated, however, if we could find a way of reducing the conflict between the new ministries and the institutional church.

Conflict with the Institutional Church

We became personally aware of this institutional conflict as we became involved in creating a new youth ministry in our own church. The form this ministry took was a free school for high school students whose needs were not being met by large, academically competitive suburban school systems.

We faced many crises. But the one crisis over which we agonized most, and which we are still working to solve, is the relationship of our own church to this new form of youth ministry.

Like so many ministries described in this book, we were forced to organize a separate corporation and to operate outside the local church. We made every attempt to keep communication channels open with the whole congregation and to develop a broad base of support. But when the project came to a vote, we were persuaded not to ask for the church's support because of the controversy and division that would ensue.

We have not given up. Some youth ministers with whom we have talked, however, have. They feel it is poor stewardship to waste their energy trying to change the institutional church when youth are waiting and willing to create their own structures. They feel that they are involved in legitimate church structures, and that the traditional church must come to accept them as such.

One youth minister said, "The church today must be a diverse church and allow the youth stuff that's going on to be an expression of the church."

But we feel that the new youth ministries have something to say to the traditional church (and vice versa), just as we feel the generations have something to say to each other. We feel that dialogue between traditional church structures and new structures could be enriching for both.

Whether this dialogue takes place within the present institutional church, or whether youth ministry moves outside and achieves its own base of power, depends to a large extent on how adaptable the present structures are to change.

And the changes being called for are radical.

Changes in the Local Church

Some of the changes called for in local churches that want to embrace a relevant youth ministry are the following.

ACCEPTING YOUTH POWER

Most youth ministers feel that youth power, or youth sharing in decisions that affect their lives, must become a reality in churches that want to develop a relevant ministry with youth.

Many ministries have moved outside the local church because youth were not allowed to share in decisions about their own ministry. Most adults are reluctant to give them this power. When they were young, these adults were considered members-in-training. They were not respected as full members of the church until they reached their twenties, had a family, and held responsible jobs in the community. They feel youth today should go through the same waiting period before assuming power and responsibility in the church.

But today's generation is demanding to have a share in the decision-making. And rightfully so. Their world is radically different from that of their parents and from the world their parents grew up in. Most adults do not know what is best for youth today. They can't give the answers; they don't even know what questions are being asked.

The statement of a leader of the Lawn-In in Melrose is one the church will have to accept: "I think we would have been way off base if it had been all adults on the committee—or all church staff. By the time we were a working committee, the kids were the leaders. They were really in touch with what was happening."

Sharing decisions in the church will not come easily. Youth may have to meet apart from the adult congregation until they

Conflict with the Institutional Church

gain enough sense of their own power to exercise it within the church (just as Blacks have separated themselves from whites in order to form a solid base of power). Youth will have to assume more responsibility for the decisions they do make.

We will have to take seriously the concerns of youth members in our churches. It is not a matter of inviting the kids to the adults' party. It is saying that the kids need to help plan the party and to determine if there will be a party at all. It means youth having a part in determining the very structure and direction of the church.

ALLOWING SOCIAL INTEGRATION

The reason most often given for new youth ministries leaving the church is the appeal they make to elements the church does not want to hold in its arms, the appeal to "those kinds of kids."

Churches have become protective of what is theirs. This includes not only buildings and property, but "their" youth. Parents are afraid that new elements attracted to the church will somehow corrupt their own children. And they are afraid of the reputation the church will gain in the community if kids with long hair, deliquents, or kids from other racial backgrounds are encouraged to come into it.

In the new ministries, however, youth have found themselves associating with the kids they were taught to fear. Barriers have been broken. Youth have discovered that underneath the veneer of cultural distinction human beings exist, human beings who love, forgive, and express themselves creatively.

Youth are finding that class is an artificial distinction we have erected to protect our values. They are finding that people who have long hair and people who are on probation and people who are poor are—underneath—just people.

Churches have put out the sign Everybody Welcome for many years. But few have really meant it. Now youth are challenging the church to accept everyone into its fellowship.

FACILITATING COMMUNITY INVOLVEMENT

For many people, the church is seen as a sanctuary from the world, a place where good people band together to live out the good life and wait for their reward in heaven.

Recently, much has been written to negate this concept of the church. Too few churches, however, have made serious attempts to move from the sanctuary into intimate involvement with their community.

Many of the new youth ministries have taken this mandate seriously. They have worked alongside, with, and in place of community organizations in meeting community needs. They have provided a Christian voice in community affairs. They have provided direct services to youth in their community. They have had a part in changing the life of the community, of making it a more human place to live.

MAKING SIGNIFICANT FINANCIAL COMMITMENTS

New youth ministries have challenged churches to commit significant funds to their ministry with youth.

In many cases, the amount the church spends in new youth ministries is much smaller than other agencies would spend on the same projects, because there are a number of committed persons within the church who are willing to work for minimal salaries or to volunteer their services. However, compared with amounts the church has spent on youth ministry in the past, the present financial needs are considerable.

These funds must come from adult members of the church, for youth are unable to support their own ministry. Our society has insured this with its emphasis on long educational careers. And as the employment market shrinks in our technological age this will be even more true.

It is always difficult to secure money for a youth ministry. We are reluctant to give funds to a ministry we cannot control and to meet needs we do not experience ourselves. We are especially reluctant to risk "throwing money away" on experimental ministries that may or may not be successful.

Yet this money is desperately needed. The needs of this generation are tremendous. And few agencies have really been involved in meeting them.

Few communities provide adequate, if any, recreational facilities for youth. Counseling services for youth are nonexistent in most communities. The self-expression of youth is bottled up in the schools and few places are provided in the community for its release.

The church has become accustomed to spending large amounts of money on its building and on its adult-oriented programs. Youth ministry has been handed only token amounts. But significant youth ministry requires significant financial commitment.

LIVING WITH CHANGE

Throughout its history, the church has not been without its innovations. The church school, now a sacred part of the establishment, was at one time a new and daring innovation. But the church, like any institution, has a way of making its innovations permanent. The more permanent they have become, the less subject they have been to change—and the less relevant they have been to the needs of the time.

The new ministries are, of necessity, temporary in nature. They grow in response to a need. When that need has passed, the program must stop, or adapt itself to some other area of need. This is particularly true in youth ministry, where the population is constantly changing and the cultural interaction is constantly creating new needs.

Churches that are involved in creative youth ministry are able and willing to live with, and support, change.

DEVELOPING A BROADER CONCEPT OF YOUTH MINISTRY

New youth ministries have broadened the concept of what youth ministry really is. Youth ministry today is more than "preparing youth to become a part of the church." It is youth, who are a part of the church now, becoming involved in mission in their world.

Youth ministry is drop-in centers, drug rehabilitation, drama groups, draft counseling. It is underground newspapers and school sit-ins. It is folk groups and new forms of worship. It is hot lines, summer recreation, and free breakfasts.

It is all of these things in addition to the study groups, retreats, and fellowships churches have traditionally held. These are still relevant expressions of youth ministry in many churches, forms that meet some of the needs of youth. But they usually do not go far enough. They serve only a small group of youth and they rarely result in real action.

A broader concept of youth ministry is being called for by persons who have experimented with new forms of youth ministry.

TAKING RISKS

Anything new, anything experimental, anything creative involves risk. The risks in new youth ministries are many, and all the fears that are raised when new directions are first suggested may be realized.

There is the risk of failure. Youth invited to a drop-in center may not come. A political activist group may not bring about significant changes in the community. Projects may never receive adequate financing. The youth minister may be wrong for the job. For various reasons, the project may fail. But failure is one of the risks that must be taken.

There are also financial risks. As one youth minister said,

Conflict with the Institutional Church

"When you have to sign the order for ninety pounds of butter for a breakfast you don't know if anyone will attend, it gets kind of lonely." But someone must assume risks like this—and even larger financial risks—if youth ministry is to be creative and relevant.

The possibility of becoming involved in controversy is always a risk in the new ministries. Controversy is present in almost any relevant ministry, but the controversy that develops in youth ministry can be very threatening, since it may result in the minister losing his job, people leaving the church, or the youth ministry being dropped. It takes courage to stand up to this kind of controversy, but this has been necessary in many of the new youth ministries.

Many churches have also faced ideological risks when they became involved in creative youth ministries. As they broadened their involvement with youth, they found their beliefs challenged, their values threatened, their ideas changed. This is a risk every thinking person should welcome, for beliefs and values that are not open to modification by experience are dogma and are probably not operative. However, it is a risk most people try to avoid. It cannot be avoided in the new youth ministries.

The ministries described in this book faced all of these risks. They would never have happened if some group had not decided that the risks were worth it. Those that failed did so for a number of reasons, but prime among them was their failure to assume risk.

A Final Word

We began this book by stating that we believed the Christian church has relevance for today's youth. We believe that youth's search for faith can find meaning in the Christian religion.

But we recognize that we no longer stand in the place of authority with the answers to all of youth's questions. We have had to humble ourselves, admit that our church institutions have sometimes failed to live out the life-style of Christ, and open ourselves to new structures and a more relevant message.

Youth are engaged in a deep search for meaning. We need to join them in this search. We need to carry on a dialogue with them, as some of the ministries described here have done. We need to develop, with youth, the forms of ministry that are appropriate to a new age.

This is a challenging task. It involves pain, risk, conflict, and sometimes failure. But to those who have tried it, it is worth all of this, because it has resulted in an abundant life for both youth and adults.

And that's what youth ministry is all about.

Appendix A

Human Relations Training Organizations (Church-Oriented)

Atlantic Christian Training Centre (United Church of Canada)
Box 159, Tatamagouche, N.S., Canada

Berkeley Center for Human Interaction (Episcopal Church)
1820 Scenic Ave., Berkeley, Calif. 94709

Black Churchmen's Ecumenical Training Facility, Inc.
1419 V St., N.W., Third Floor, Washington, D.C. 20009

Center for Creative Living and Spiritual Growth
Brookside, Beech Haven, Athens, Ga. 30601

Center for Parish Development at Evangelical Theological Seminary (United Methodist)
329 E. School Ave., Naperville, Ill. 60540

Consultant/Trainers Southwest: Southwest Training Lab
c/o Texas Conference of Churches, 1400 Guadalupe, Austin, Tex. 78701

Cranbrook Center for Human Resources
380 Lone Pine Rd., Bloomfield Hills, Mich. 48013

Ecumenical Continuing Education Center at Yale
363 St. Ronan St., New Haven, Conn. 06511

Ecumenical Institute (A Division of the Church Federation of Greater Chicago)
3444 W. Congress Pkwy., Chicago, Ill. 60624

Human Relations Training Organizations

Ecumenical Institute: Detroit
Box 1233, Detroit, Mich. 48231

Ecumenical Institute: New York City
250 Everit St., New Haven, Conn. 06511

Educational Center for Research and Consultation
6357 Clayton Rd., St. Louis, Mo. 63117

Episcopal Diocese of Olympia
1551 Tenth Ave., E., Seattle, Wash. 98102

Foundation for Religion and Mental Health, Inc.
185 E. 85th St., Suite 35K, New York, N.Y. 10028

Lancaster Theological Seminary, The Center for Human Development and Continuing Education
519 James St., Lancaster, Pa. 17603

Lands End–New York Synod Center for Renewal and Study
Star Route 109, Box 5, Saranac Lake, N.Y. 12923

Malta Institute–All Saints' Episcopal School
Vicksburg, Miss. 39180

Michigan Episcopal Training Network
740 Church Rd., Bloomfield Hills, Mich. 48013

Midwest Ecumenical Training Associates
65 E. Huron St., Chicago, Ill. 60611

National Training Center for Human Relations and Design Skills (United Methodist)
Box 871, Nashville, Tenn. 37202

Pendle Hill: Quaker Center for Study and Contemplation
Wallingford, Pa. 19086

Prairie Christian Training Centre (United Church of Canada)
159 Fort Qu'Appelle, Sask., Canada

Prairie View Mental Health Center (Mennonite)
Box 467, Newton, Kan. 67114

Princeton Seminary Continuing Education Center
12 Library Pl., Princeton, N.J. 08540

St. Paul School of Theology–Center for Renewal
Truman Rd. and VanBrunt Blvd., Kansas City, Mo. 64127

SEARCH
1 Campus Dr., Box 141 Madison, N.J. 07940

Synod of Florida
Conference Center, Route 2, Box 230, Lake Placid, Fla. 33852

Virginia Theological Seminary (Center for Continuing Education)
Alexandria, Va. 22304

Yokefellow Institute
920 Earlham Dr., Richmond, Ind. 47274

Appendix B

Action Training Organizations (Members of the Action Training Coalition)

ACTS: Association for Christian Training Services
692 Poplar Ave., Memphis, Tenn. 38105
Contact person: William A. Jones, Jr.

BCETF: Black Churchmen's Ecumenical Training Facility, Inc.
1419 V St., N.W., Third Floor, Washington, D. C. 20009
Contact person: Charles W. Green

CATA: Columbus Action Training Associates
79 E. State St., Room 814, Columbus, Ohio 43215
Contact person: Jon K. Brown

CATS: Community Action Training Services
9606 Euclid Ave., Cleveland, Ohio 44106
Contact person: Robert H. Bonthius

CHART: Community Human and Resources Training
208 Calhoun St., Cincinnati, Ohio 45221
Contact person: Paul Henry

COMMIT: Center for Metropolitan Mission In-Service
817 W. 34th St., Los Angeles, Calif. 90007
Contant person: Speed Leas

CUE: (Portland) Center for Urban Encounter
0245 S.W. Bancroft St., Portland, Ore. 97201
Contant person: Paul J. Schulze

Action Training Organizations

CUE: (Twin Cities) Center for Urban Encounter
3338 University Avenue, W. E., Minneapolis, Minn. 55414
Contact person: William Grace

CUT: Canadian Urban Training Project for Christian Service
875 Queen St., Toronto 8, Ont., Canada
Contact person: Ed File

GLIDE: Glide Urban Center
330 Ellis St., San Francisco, Calif., 94102
Contact person: Lewis E. Durham

ICUA: Inter-Religious Center for Urban Affairs
Shell Bldg., Suite 811, 1221 Locust St., St. Louis, Mo. 63103
Contact person: Jack Quigley

JOUM: Joint Office for Urban Ministry
841 Genesee St., Rochester, N.Y. 14619
Contact person: Larry Coppard

METC: Metropolitan Ecumenical Training Center, Inc
1419 V St., N.W. Washington, D.C. 20009
Contact person: Tilden Edwards, Jr.

MTN: Midwest Training Network
3210 Michigan, Kansas City, Mo. 64109
Contact person: Bob Beech

MUST: Metropolitan Urban Service Training, Inc.
235 G. 49th St., New York, N.Y. 10017
Contact person: George Younger

PIIR: Presbyterrian Institute of Industrial Relations
800 W. Belden Ave., Chicago, Ill. 60614
Contact person: James Armstrong

PRISA: Urban Training Center for Caribbean Area
Diocese of Puerto Rico, Box 9002, Santurce, P.R. 00908
Contact person: Alfonso Roman

TRUST: Task Force for Research, Urban Strategy and Training, Inc.
Box 1312, Richmond, Va. 23210
Contact person: Richard Perkins

UTC: Urban Training Center
400 N. Ashland Ave., Chicago, Ill. 60607
Contact person: James P. Morton

UTOA: Urban Training Organization of Atlanta, Inc.
1026 Ponce de Leon Ave., N.W., Atlanta, Ga. 30306
Contact person: Edgar Grider

UYAA: Urban Young Adult Action
74 Trinita Pl., 11th Floor, New York, N.Y. 10006
Contact person: Earl Barr

Appendix C

Sources of Information on Foundation Grants

The Foundation Directory
Publications Department
Russell Sage Foundation
230 Park Ave.
New York, N.Y. 10017 (Price: $12)

A list of over 6,000 foundations with the corporate name and address, date and form of organization, name of donor or donors, general purpose and activities, special limitations, assets, gifts received, expenditures and grants for the most recent available year, and names of officers and trustees.

Foundation News (published bimonthly)
The Foundation Center
444 Madison Ave.
New York, N.Y., 10022   (Price: $6 per year)

News and articles about foundations plus a report on foundation grants. Grants for religion, health, and welfare are listed in January and July.

The Foundation Center and Its Depository Libraries

(990–A forms are available in these libraries, listing grants from individual foundations.)

Sources of Information on Foundation Grants

Library	*Forms on file for:*
The Foundation Center 444 Madison Ave. New York, N.Y. 10022 (Mrs. Ewa Pascoe)	all states and D.C.
The Foundation Center 1001 Connecticut Ave., N. W. Washington, D. C. 20036 (Mrs. Margot Brinkley)	all states and D.C.
Graduate Social Science Library Stephens Hall University of California Berkeley, Calif. 94720 (Richard V. Teggert) (Miss Geraldine Scalzo)	California, Idaho, Nevada, Oregon, Washington
Foundation Collection Reference Department University of California University Research Library Los Angeles, Calif. 90024 (Mrs. Ann T. Hinckley)	Arizona, California
Foundation Library Collection Atlanta Public Library 126 Carnegie Way, N. W. Atlanta, Ga. 30303 (Miss Isabel Ehrlich)	Alabama, Florida, Georgia, Mississippi, North Carolina, South Carolina, Tennessee
The Newberry Library 60 W. Walton St. Chicago, Ill. 60610 (Arthur H. Miller)	Illinois
Danforth Foundation Library	Kansas, Missouri

222 S. Central Ave.
St. Louis, Mo. 63105
  (Dr. Gene L. Schwilck)

Cleveland Foundation Library   Ohio
700 National City Bank Building
Cleveland, Ohio 44114
  (Mrs. Elise van Bergen)

Regional Foundation Library   Arkansas, Louisiana,
The Hogg Foundation
for Mental Health   New Mexico, Oklahoma,
University of Texas   Texas
Austin, Tex. 78712
  (Mrs. Dorothe Bozza)

THANKS TO

· all who helped us find new forms of youth ministry.
· all who shared with us their new forms of youth ministry.
· Vergie Gillespie and Dr. Arthur Crabtree for critiquing the manuscript.
· Claryce Johnson for support and encouragement.
· Gracie Adkins for research assistance.
· Anna Jacobs and Gloria Kaminski for transcribing tapes.